Faith in the World

Faith in the World

*Mark Gibbs and Vesper Society,
Being God's Lively People*

By Nelvin Vos, Daniel Pryfogle and Melvin George

A Vesper Society Imprint

This book was supported by Vesper Society as a gift in gratitude to Robert Brorby, passionate advocate for the ministry of the laity, on the occasion of his retirement from the Board of Directors in 2006 after almost forty years of leadership within the Society. It is dedicated to him, to the Society's founders, Gene Heckathorn (in memoriam) and Bob Cummings, to George Spindt, longtime Society leader, and to all who followed them in exemplifying the words of Mark Gibbs, quoted by Robert Brorby in a tribute after Gibbs' death: "[W]e must hold to the great truth that God calls us … in everything we do … Nothing is exempt, until the hour of our death."

"Our vocation – the vocation of all human beings – is the call from God to be part of the new humanity in Jesus Christ, to be citizens of the Kingdom and the People of God. And this is true for *all* of us, whatever our occupation and job, and indeed whether we are employed or not. This marvelous vocation and dignity is for everybody, irrespective of our age, sex, education, race, nationality, intellectual ability, occupation – or ordination."

– *Mark Gibbs, "Vocation, Work, and Work for Pay,"* Word and World, *1984*

❧ Contents ❧

Preface and Acknowledgments

This book has gone through a metamorphosis of both its authorship and its content. It began as an effort by Nelvin Vos to write a biography of Mark Gibbs. Through discussion with Mary Baich, president of Vesper Society, and Melvin George, a Society board member, the focus broadened to the convergence of Mark Gibbs and Vesper Society within the larger context of what today is called the ministry in daily life movement. Daniel Pryfogle, a consultant to Vesper Society, was enlisted to explore the Society's rich contributions both in this country and abroad over its more than forty-year history. George offered to coordinate the efforts of these two major authors of the book and to contribute to the Introduction and to Chapter 5. So this has been very much a group effort.

Although we each drafted individual portions of the book, we all critiqued and revised the full manuscript. And many people helped us in substantial ways. We especially acknowledge the support and contributions of ...

- Mary Baich and the Board of Directors of Vesper Society for their encouragement and underwriting of the project;

- Carol McKevitt, project associate of Vesper Society, for finding important details in the archives of the organization;

- Robert Cummings, Robert Brorby, and George Spindt for many conversations about their memories of Mark Gibbs and of the past and present work of the Society;

- The staff of the John Rylands Library of the University of Manchester for their assistance to Vos and George in researching the papers of Mark Gibbs; and Dr. Karl Krueger of the Krauth Memorial Library of The Lutheran Theological Seminary at Philadelphia, who provided several resources for the manuscript;

- Lee Langan, former Vesper Hayward Hospital board member, for the use of his photographs of Mark Gibbs;

- Joel Thoreson, chief archivist for the Evangelical Lutheran Church in America, for his assistance in locating important documents about Mark Gibbs' work with the denomination;

- Robert Brorby, Mary Baich, Vesper Society Vice President Sabrina Lynn Motley, and former board member Ted Carlstrom for reading the manuscript in draft form and for offering helpful suggestions;

- And the many others cited in the text who contributed insights.

We are grateful to all who were involved in this undertaking. We have attempted to work as carefully as possible with the sources available to us, but any errors of fact or interpretation are ours.

Our journey together has been meaningful. Reading Mark Gibbs, delving into the history of Vesper Society, and asking critical questions about the relevance of their collaboration for today has sparked passionate conversations among us three. We hope our readers are similarly inspired and that their resulting reflections may prove to be important not only for Vesper Society but for the larger ministry in daily life movement.

Nelvin Vos
Daniel Pryfogle
Melvin George

December 2008

❧ Introduction ❧

On May 14, 1965, in a Philadelphia bar and grill, two successful businessmen came up with a novel idea.

They had spent the day consulting with Lutheran institutions in the city at the request of Dr. Franklin Clark Fry, first president of the Lutheran Church in America (LCA). Gene Heckathorn was the founder and president of an agricultural chemical corporation in Richmond, California, and Bob Cummings was a consultant in the development and management of senior housing and earlier had been a co-partner in a firm that fabricated steel pressure vessels. Both businessmen had long been active lay leaders in one of the LCA's predecessor church bodies, serving on various boards and councils, and they had become good friends after meeting at the 1964 LCA national convention in Harrisburg, Pennsylvania.

Cummings and Heckathorn were among those laypersons asked by Dr. Fry to assist various church-related institutions in the complicated period of transition to the new denomination. They found that many of the church's institutions, especially social service agencies, including hospitals and other healthcare agencies, had management problems that their business experience could address. They came to realize that they were *doing ministry* as lay Christians in new settings, as they applied their skills and experiences in the world outside the congregation.

Their dinner meeting in Philadelphia came after a busy day of working with a Lutheran home for the aged, among other church-related institutions, and as they were relaxing at dinner they compared notes on their varied assignments from Dr. Fry. It occurred to the two business-men that many other laypeople would also gladly use their abilities and knowledge in similar ministry in new ways, so they dreamed of forming a nonprofit corporation that would provide management services and consultation to church-related institutions and

Eugene Heckathorn

other nonprofit agencies. They anticipated staffing the organization by networking with other laypersons throughout the U.S., "persons of var-ied talents" who were "agreeable to respond on an as-needed basis with small honoraria and expenses," as Cummings later put it.

Excitedly, the two friends sketched out the organizational chart of this new corporation on the back of a placemat at The Vesper Bar and Grill. Observing that the establishment's name sounded rather religious (though its function was quite dif-ferent!), the men decided to call the organization Vesper Society – "society" in keeping with their networking notion for the staffing of the effort.

Robert Cummings

Less than two months later, Vesper Society was incorporated in the state of California. Heckathorn wrote in his journal on July 2, 1965:

> Today the Vesper Society was organized. A nonprofit charitable organization to do good works for man. Why would we do something like this? Those that heard couldn't quite accept it – charity should be done by charitable organizations – older ones that is – by the church – certainly not by crass commercial types like us.

> ... I think I can do more for people than all the "do-gooders" I know – at least we are going to try.

It was an amazing and bold idea for that era – that two church laymen could use their business talents and experience in Christian service, not within the church organization itself but in the world beyond.

At about the same time, a third man, The Rev. George Spindt, enters the story, destined to play a key role in the events described in this book. Spindt had been a friend of Cummings since they were young children. As teenagers, the two boys occasionally assisted the pastor of their Pasadena congregation with the liturgy. Later, their paths crossed again, when Spindt had a job in hospital administration, which he resigned to go into the armed forces. Cummings took his place at the hospital, but Spindt flunked the physical exam for the military, went instead to seminary, and was ordained.

In 1949-1950, Spindt worked in Germany as director of resettlement for the Lutheran World Federation's refugee services, based in Frankfurt. There he was in the midst of conversations about how the church in Germany had failed to resist the rise of Nazism and, more generally, about the role of the church's laypeople in such social and political movements.

Later, Spindt moved from Southern California to Redwood City (in the San Francisco Bay Area), to become pastor of Messiah Lutheran Church. While in Southern California, Spindt had joined the board of Pacoima Memorial Lutheran Hospital, an institution founded after a plane crash in a neighborhood that had no hospital in which to treat victims of the crash. So Spindt had been deeply involved in a hospital established out of concern for the underserved.

Near Spindt's new residence in Redwood City, a hospital in San Leandro was struggling financially, and through a family connection between a Pacoima board member and the group of Lutherans who had established the San Leandro hospital, Pacoima offered to help the other institution, eventually acquiring the San Leandro facility. Thus Spindt, as the only Pacoima board member in Northern California, naturally became involved in the affairs of its new subsidiary in San Leandro.

In addition to his long friendship with Cummings, Spindt also knew Heckathorn well through their shared activities in the Pacific Southwest Synod of the Lutheran Church in America. When the Bank of California, which held a large note from the San Leandro hospital, became uneasy about the loan, Heckathorn and Cummings, the two founders of Vesper Society, were asked in 1966 to assist in the management of the hospital. Soon Vesper Society itself took over formal management responsibility and eventually, in 1969, became the owner of the San Leandro hospital. So Heckathorn and Cummings and Spindt were now all three, together with Vesper Society, involved in this hospital work in San Leandro. At almost the same time, these three were joined by attorney Robert Brorby, who had met Heckathorn through their work in the church and was recruited by him to join the Vesper Society Board of Directors in 1967. Brorby played a major role in many of the events of this book.

It was Spindt who provided the link between Vesper Society and Mark Gibbs, a very significant – some might say providential – connection. In the mid-1960s, Cliff Weihe, a member of Spindt's Redwood City staff, while on an extended trip to Europe, had met Gibbs, a prominent Anglican layman. Gibbs was an active spokesman for the role of the laity in society and in the church, and had many international contacts, particularly with the German Kirchentag, a major laity gathering, and with the Association of Lay Centres in Europe. So he was closely connected with the postwar movement in Europe to encourage laypeople to carry their faith into the secular arenas of society.

Gibbs had recently (1964) co-authored with T. Ralph Morton the book *God's Frozen People*, which deeply impressed Weihe in its call for the active involvement of Christian laypeople in the work of the world.

So he invited Gibbs to Redwood City for a week of seminars. Gibbs did come to California, and his series of lectures in Redwood City eventually resulted in another book, *God's Lively People.*

Gene Heckathorn had intended to provide Spindt with a trip to Europe to thank him for his role in the transition of the San Leandro hospital to Vesper Society but also to make contacts for the Society in Europe through the connections Spindt had made during his refugee resettlement work with LWF in 1949-1950. When Spindt told Gibbs about Heckathorn's plan to send him to Europe, Gibbs offered

Mark Gibbs

to help, since he had much more current connections with the European laity movement.

Spindt did go to Europe in July 1969. He remembers being at the Stuttgart Kirchentag, at the urging of Gibbs to connect with this German lay movement, when the U.S. moon landing was announced on July 20, 1969. He and his wife, the only Americans on a trolley in Stuttgart, were applauded by the other passengers after the announcement of the landing came!

During a subsequent return trip to Redwood City, Gibbs was urged by Spindt to talk to Heckathorn, in part because Heckathorn's soul-searching about his chemical company's role in the Vietnam War had led to his deep reflection on the role of a Christian layperson in the work of the world. Spindt felt that Heckathorn and Gibbs would have much in common, given their mutual interest in the role of Christian laity in the affairs and structures of the world. At the time, Heckathorn was in Oregon on extended business involving a milling company that a Catholic group had inherited, for which they needed management help. Gibbs agreed to go to Oregon, and there followed a second key dinner in the Society's history, this one in Portland on May 17, 1970.

Gibbs and Heckathorn had a vigorous conversation that night about ways in which they might work together to advance their joint concern about mobilizing laity to do the work of God in the secular world from a Christian perspective. Gibbs was very much a networker himself, having moved around Europe and the U.S., bringing people together to talk, sometimes about a particular topic, but often with no specific agenda and certainly no pre-determined outcome. So he resonated with the "society" concept that had been expressed by Cummings and Heckathorn during their Philadelphia dinner; indeed, Gibbs himself had referred to the church as a "society." Later, Gibbs wrote this account of that encounter with Heckathorn:

> It was a memorable occasion. For several hours, with his own particular kind of Churchillian rhetoric, he bombarded me with his visions and plans for Vesper Society. It was to do far more than run a hospital in San Leandro: it was to become a national, nay more an international movement. It was to develop a major program of health care centers. It was to develop the potentials of church laypeople. ... It must have its own, prestigious, well-printed magazine; and I must edit it. Indeed I personally must work on all these plans: it was the most important thing I could possibly do. Would I help him? Would I dare not to? I waited, and occasionally managed to slip in a short question; and sometime late in the evening the great monologue began to slow down a little. I promised Gene that I would give him some sort of answer at breakfast the next morning.

After a night of wondering whether he could, "as something of an English intellectual, really work together with this very determined Californian Christian tycoon," Gibbs responded to Heckathorn at breakfast that he would attempt to help Vesper Society with its international programs, with its seminars and its work with church laypeople, with its future thinking and planning. But he saw the glossy publication as completely unrealistic, and suggested a much more informal "exchange," a collection of reprints of material from the pages of English-language publications here and abroad. That was the origin of what was called *Vesper Exchange*.

Thus was completed the transition from a radical idea sketched out by two Christian laymen on a placemat in Philadelphia in 1965 to an organization in 1970 owning a hospital and now formally connected with an international advocate and spokesman for the Christian ministry of the laity in the world. In the 1970 first issue of *Vesper Exchange*, Gibbs wrote a piece titled "Our First Priority" in which he expressed in new words the tone Vesper Society wished to set:

> In fact the main vocation of God's people is not to build
> and to support church structures (though some of these
> may certainly be necessary). It is to find a new style of
> humanity – in explicitly Christian terms to be the Body
> of Christ, the intelligent and committed embodiment of
> Christian love and service – *in the secular structures in
> which God has placed or will place them.*"

The convergence of Mark Gibbs and Vesper Society, in the context of postwar concern about the role of the laity, produced an organization now almost a half-century old that continues the commitments of its founders to doing God's work through the secular structures that were not, in the mind of Gibbs, separated from the sacred but very much a part of God's world, too. The general purpose of Vesper Society has remained unchanged – to do God's work as laypeople, through organizations that operate both efficiently and humanely, in order to create a more compassionate world.

That purpose captures the hope shared by many laypeople around the world. Such Christians, whose passion has been manifested across church history and was reignited in the 20th century, constitute a movement that has sought to claim daily life, with all of its relationships, systems, and structures, as the realm of Christian ministry. To read Vesper Society's history is to glimpse this larger movement.

Faith in the World explores the connection between Vesper Society – which began at a 1965 dinner in Philadelphia – and Mark Gibbs, who became connected with Vesper Society at a 1970 dinner in Portland. The title *Faith in the World* suggests both the confidence that the major players in our story had in laypeople and in secular institutions as well as their strong desire to apply their Christian faith to the betterment of the world.

The book begins with the life and work of Mark Gibbs. Chapter 2 explores the vision Vesper Society shared with Gibbs, who became an ambassador for the Society on ministry of the laity. Chapter 3 describes in greater detail the way Gibbs worked to advance his vision for the laity, right up to the end of his life, while Chapter 4 focuses on how Vesper Society expanded its activities before and following Gibbs' death in 1986 – and how that work reflected the changing understandings of ministry in daily life. Finally, the book concludes with Chapter 5, which explores insights for the future that might be drawn from the Gibbs-Vesper convergence.

By exploring that convergence, the context in which Vesper Society and Gibbs worked together, and the catalytic effect of their sixteen-year conversation on the role of laity in the world and on the development of the Society, we hope this book will not only illuminate the past but also suggest possibilities for the ministry in daily life movement and Vesper Society in a future in which the societal role and influence of the church-as-institution is changing quite substantially.

1

A Voice from and to the Laity

His Calling

This story could well begin in flight. Mark Gibbs is crossing the Atlantic in December 1981, returning home to England after his inaugural Vesper/Audenshaw Laity Lecture in San Francisco and Chicago. He has been appealing for the "development of a strong and committed laity," by which he means Christians "who are committed to God's will as revealed in Jesus Christ, and to that will not only on Sunday and in our private religion, not only in church affairs, but also in the whole spectrum of our lives' activities." His words are familiar to those who have read his books and essays or heard him speak before. He is blunt and provocative.

Thirty-six years have passed since the end of World War II and the beginning of a resurgent movement of laity in the church. Looking back, Gibbs sees some progress in the theological understanding that all Christians are "called to a high quality of life in Christ Jesus – not just clergy, and not just church workers ..." But he sees failure as well. Laypeople, he argues, have been sloppy and simplistic in their thinking about pressing social issues. Without quality education and discipleship for laypeople, they are "too often left in ignorance, to twitch or stagger, as it were, emotionally, when there comes a new crisis, a new problem, a new disaster." The church, he contends, has failed to achieve a real partnership between clergy and laity because the institution is so focused on its own maintenance and, consequently, does not affirm lay ministry other than volunteer service that occurs on the premises of the church. So laypeople feel isolated in their daily lives, unsupported for their vocation in the world.

This is the reality that Gibbs carries with him everywhere he travels and now as he returns home to his small cottage in the English countryside. He is like a missionary of old, chasing the movement of the Spirit in the world but frustrated that the church is not keeping up. His patience wears thin. The sense of loneliness is real. He understands the weariness that others feel, their loss of enthusiasm. But he also knows the cost of Christian discipleship – a cost, he says, that is measured "not only in time and money, but also sometimes in pain and in uncomfortable living." And so he travels on, trusting in God's grace. He cannot do otherwise. This is his calling.

For sixteen years, Gibbs' journey intersected with Vesper Society. During this time Gibbs became a visible expression of the Society's commitment to the ministry of the laity. In his speaking and writing, in the U.S. and abroad, he challenged laypeople to live their Christian faith in all areas of their experience. And the Society provided much of the support to amplify his unique voice – a voice from and to the laity. Throughout his life, his perspective was that of a layperson. He was "forever unordained and forever content to so remain," as one writer put it.

Born on April 4, 1920, Gibbs was a student at St. Dunstan's College in East London from 1931-1937 and graduated with honors from the University College of London in 1940, the same year that Germany commenced its air blitz of London. Details of Gibbs' life during the war are scarce, but in 1946 he began teaching history and economics at Audenshaw Grammar School (in American terms, a tax-supported high school) in Manchester. Eventually, he became the head of his department and held this post until 1964. That an intensely private, bachelor school teacher should become one of the 20th century's foremost leaders in the movement for ministry of the laity is an extraordinary story.

Already in the early 1950s, Gibbs was involved in several laity organizations. He gave prominent leadership to the Christian Frontier Council, a British network founded by Joseph Oldham in 1942 to support Christian leaders on "the frontline of the battle" to make Christianity a living faith in the world. Soon after the war, Gibbs visited German and Austrian refugee camps. These visits prompted his first ecumenical venture, the Audenshaw Periodical Service, which distributed donated publications to the camps and later to Third World colleges. In 1954 he returned to Germany to attend the Leipzig Kirchentag. Four years later, Gibbs was elected chair of the International Committee of the Kirchentag, a post he held for 20 years.

Gibbs was deeply influenced by the Iona Community, a Christian ecumenical center on the Isle of Iona off Scotland. Begun in 1938 by George MacLeod on the foundations of a medieval Benedictine abbey, Iona's mission captured Gibbs' imagination: "A Christian ecumenical community working for peace and social justice, the rebuilding of community, and the renewal of worship." Iona was envisioned as an "experiment in partnership" between young clergy and industrial workers. MacLeod's description of this well-known center surely resonated with Gibbs' integration of faith and life; Iona was a "thin place – only a tissue paper separating the material from the spiritual," MacLeod said.

In 1955 Gibbs presented a week of lectures at Iona on the ministry of the laity, part of a summer series for new Iona members and visitors. The invitation came from T. Ralph Morton, the community's deputy leader and an ordained minister in the Church of Scotland who had earlier been involved in laity education in China and had been at Iona since 1943. The two became close friends and partners in dialogue, engaging others in conversation at Iona and elsewhere over the next eight years. After Gibbs resigned his teaching position in 1964, and while serving as associate secretary of lay centers in Europe, Gibbs and Morton founded the Audenshaw Foundation (named after Gibbs' school). Its "fundamental objective" was "to encourage the support, education and development of the laity – in all the churches and outside them – as they struggled to understand and apply the Christian faith in the everyday world of today and tomorrow." Among its activities was the publishing of the Audenshaw Papers, which concentrated on "the concerns of the laity in social and secular affairs" and the Audenshaw Documents "for specialists in laity education." Gibbs often reprinted excerpts from these publications later under the auspices of Vesper Society.

Gibbs and Morton's collaboration led to the provocative book *God's Frozen People*, published in 1964. Gibbs and Morton used the book as a springboard for two weekly series of lectures at Iona: in August 1965 on the theme "Tension in a Changing Church – the Loyalties and Sympathies of the Laity"; and in July 1968 centering on "The Layman's Education." The book catapulted Gibbs onto the international stage of church renewal and signaled the major themes he would later develop more fully in his writing and speaking.

Gibbs and Morton declared that the church is the laity, the whole people of God. The church is not an institution that needs people to serve it or maintain it, they said. While it requires some structure, the church is "essentially people living a life together: the people of God living the life of Christ." Herein lies the church's mystery:

> It is a divine society, not because of an infallible doctrine or an incorruptible organization, but because Jesus called [people] to follow him, and still does. It is not a religious society. It is a lay society because it is made up

of the men and women Jesus calls. ...

Because God is from the beginning at work in his world, because, in the life and death and resurrection of Jesus Christ, he brought his creation to a new stage and in terms of a man, a human being, because his creative work still goes on through his Spirit in [people] and in the world – because of this fundamental belief we know that the church is the mystery of God's creation: a church made up of men and women, the only true lay, secular society, the herald and the instrument of God's purpose for all mankind.

The book's central thesis is that churches are too often inwardly drawn and do not pay attention to the work of ministry in the world. Such a church is a "cozy group" – "a little local holy huddle," Gibbs later wrote. Instead, he and Morton insisted, "God's Holy Spirit is given to his people not for the running of a 'happy fellowship' of Sunday and weeknight evening activities, but for the agonizing work of serving – 'ministering to' ... the needs of others." They added: "[I]f there has to be a choice between upsetting some of God's faithful veterans in the congregations or failing to serve some of God's frozen and lonely people on the fringe of our churches, then it seems to us clear which is the choice we must make, according to all that the New Testament teaches." Later they put the matter even more bluntly: "Indeed, the first duty of the layman in his local church is to be a nuisance."

And Gibbs' future work was often just that: to be "an extremely useful nuisance," as one writer put it. William Diehl, a prominent Lutheran advocate for the ministry of the laity, writing after Gibbs' death, said, "Mark cherished the role of being the lay curmudgeon in matters of the church ..." Gibbs took seriously the task of not only comforting the afflicted but afflicting the comfortable.

He ranted about how the church's budget priorities for educating the clergy overwhelm the need to equip the laity in their daily ministry:

"It is also unfortunate – and rather extraordinary – that the very people who are on the frontline of secular decision-making and (maybe) compromising and politicking are those for whom the churches provide the *least* opportunity for adult Christian education, for intelligent spiritual formation, and for self-development as mature and reasonably confident believers." And he often exhorted laity not to be so dependent on clergy. As Robert Brorby, longtime Vesper Society leader, has said:

> Mark was perceived by many as a critic of the institutional church – and that he was – often with a sharp tongue or pen. But his criticism was based on his frustration with the institution's concentration on "churchy" matters and the institution's failure to understand that the church in mission and ministry is primarily the Christian layperson in the secular world at work and at leisure. But he affirmed the church as both community and institution, the necessity of individual worship, prayer and evangelism, and the ministry of "churchless Christians" who had expressed dissatisfaction with the institutional church by "voting with their feet."

Gibbs' memorable distinction between Type A and Type B laity is representative of his perceptive thinking. Type A are the "worldly" laity whose interest in service lies outside the church's buildings, while Type B are "churchy" laity who focus their service on the church's premises and activities. Although he made clear that the church needs some Type B people to sustain the institution, he pleaded for the education of Type A people to help them find an answer to the question: What difference does the Christian faith make in our daily lives? Or, as he phrased it, "Why should a scientist or engineer or administrator attach any great importance to religion unless it says in the work you are doing day by day, you are a partner of God in His work of creation and to the realization of His purpose?"

Gibbs' calling to advocate for and challenge the laity characterized his entire life of witness and service. Many individuals and organizations recognized his pioneering work, including Iowa Wesleyan College, which awarded Gibbs an honorary Doctor of Humane Letters at its opening convocation in September 1967. Dr. Franklin Littell, then president of the college, was a close associate of Gibbs; he had preceded Gibbs as chair of the International Committee of the Kirchentag. Gibbs had also served as a consultant to the Lay Training Project, which the college initiated. The college's citation summed up Gibbs' work and influence:

> Mark Gibbs, as teacher and journalist, you have demonstrated professional skill. As ecumenical leader and layman of the new style, you have shown imagination and courage. Your co-authorship of *God's Frozen People*, like your editorships, has inspired and guided thousands ... You have advanced the cause of the lay apostolate by hard work and faithfulness.

With characteristic directness, Gibbs responded by offering a description of four types of laypeople:

> Those who will not face that they no longer live in the 16th century; those who have been alienated from the church after being insulted, brainwashed, or forced into an obedience they cannot take; those who are unconvinced and uncommitted, but stand independently apart; and those who are convinced that the Gospel is relevant to tomorrow, but in new ways.

Gibbs dedicated his life to those in the last category – laypeople looking for new ways to be faithful followers of Christ in the secular world where they lived.

The Person

Gibbs' home was in what he called his "Corner Cottage" in Muker, a small village nestled amid the hills of North Yorkshire. Muker provided Gibbs with the solitude he wanted and needed. Robert Brorby recalled the small, picturesque village:

> You drove to the right of the narrow two-lane road just beyond the churchyard and then the buildings were arranged in the shape of a crescent. Mark's home was on the upside of the hill with nothing but tall grass – not lawn, a few trees and structures and the hill behind. You would drive by the entire "residential" area in a matter of seconds.

Gibbs immensely enjoyed the surrounding countryside and frequently took walks around the area made famous by the author James Herriot in *All Things Great and Small*. One of these walks of about two miles from the village led to what Gibbs called "Crackpot Hall." Brorby recounted how "it was not an easy place to get to – the only access being

Violet Brorby, wife of longtime Vesper Society leader Robert Brorby, stands outside Mark Gibbs' Muker cottage.

a hike across the meadows and up the hill behind the Muker houses." And Spindt recalled how the journey went over countless stiles as one crossed the dale. The destination was an abandoned stone building somewhat in ruin. Only Gibbs' closest acquaintances were invited to the walk, since upon arrival, Gibbs, while standing amid the rubble, ritualistically welcomed them into "the secret order of the Crackpot Club" and later presented a certificate to verify their membership. "Mark would always refer to the club with glee on his face and in his voice," Brorby said. "And no one could be member unless he – and I think they were all he's – had made the pilgrimage to the site. I never knew how many persons had been elevated to this supreme status."

Michael Taylor, a close friend of Gibbs who chaired the Audenshaw Foundation for some time, described the charm of the writer's home: "We visited the cottage in Muker many times and walked the dales with Mark. The cottage was full of books wall-to-wall and even over the tops of the doors. Tiny and warm upstairs and cold and damp downstairs where we slept with our children. We had a good time but always went home with colds!"

Gibbs regarded his home as a haven and "an earthly heaven," said Bruce Johnson, who served on Vesper Society's staff through the mid-1980s. "He spoke of being exhausted mentally and emotionally from his travels and efforts," Johnson recalled, "but there he could and did apparently collapse, in his own words, 'in tears of relief before blessed sleep.'"

Johnson visited Muker and the cottage once. "[T]he circumstances were a bit unusual," he said.

> [W]hen I got to Mark's village (being fairly sure he wasn't there), I stopped at the village post, located where else but in the local pub, to ask of him. 'Oh, yes, Mr. Gibbs [is] not here, but you'll find his place just up the hill from the church, down the right lane and up the left lane, you won't miss it, sort of hobbit house appearing.' I started to leave, thanking him, when much to my surprise, he added: 'Go in, if you like, it always appears all shut up, but he never bars the door.' My interest, curiosity, and desire to experience something more of this strange man overcame my respect for privacy, especially his privacy. Entering, I had two sensations: how small, compact it was; and, anywhere there was not a table, chair, sink, toilet, bed, there were BOOKS. Floor to

ceiling, wall to wall, above the sink, in closets. All
arranged and most with some appearance of good use.

Johnson wanted to stay longer, but "a mystique of awe" came over him,
he said, and he closed the unbarred door. "Maybe it was holiness ... of
the Gibbsian type, of course!"

Once, when Spindt and his wife were visiting Gibbs, the front door
opening onto the street was ajar. Some overly curious tourist peered in
and exclaimed, "Ah! The village library!" "Mark was not amused,"
Spindt said. But the out-of-the-way village fit Gibbs "like a glove," said
Brorby, who added,

> He undoubtedly became the village squire – the one
> from The City; he had no colleagues there since the
> populace were country folk, not scholars. Probably the
> village priest or parson was the closest he would come to
> sophistication. He genuinely liked the people and he
> went there for the solitude. He could take walks in the
> countryside; he could read, think, and write to his
> heart's content.

And he did write, not only at Muker but also during his travels. The
writings and correspondence are now housed in the archives of the John
Rylands Library of the University of Manchester. The archives are doc-
umented on sixty-three single-spaced pages.

Gibbs' writing and speaking were a reflection of his own practice as a
Christian. Laity need to be "strong and committed," he said in a 1981 lecture. He challenged his audience by quoting Dr. Elliott Bradley of the
Vancouver School of Theology: "God's grace comes to us as we dare to
take on more than we can manage." Gibbs added: "We laity, like our clergy partners, can grow in strength only when we dare to take on a little
more – not the whole world, but a little bit more than we are comfortable
with. Spiritual growth comes from a certain style of Christian courage."
Gibbs displayed such courage when he castigated the church for turning

inward and not being involved in calling believers to live their faith in the world. This courage is upheld by what Gibbs called "the incredible generosity of God, who does not grudgingly bless us because we mention the name of Jesus Christ or something like that, but who is aching for us to be partners with him in our lives." Later, he wrote:

> If only we can understand, if only the clergy taught us more about the incredible *eagerness* of God, as shown by Jesus Christ, to bless us, to help us, to put our lives straight, to lead us through the dangerous jobs and murky political swamps and give us courage for the tough and messy business of modern living. This is his grace, his loving generosity.

Gibbs' temper could be short. George Spindt recalled Gibbs' anger when he learned that his lectures at Messiah Lutheran Church in Redwood City had been taped. Gibbs intended the presentations to be a resource for his next book, *God's Lively People*. Spindt destroyed the tapes. "He had ways of making you feel stupid," Spindt said. "He was very blunt." But Gibbs also possessed a great sense of humor. At the wine parties following the Redwood City lectures, he insisted that every guest who used the word "church" pay a twenty-five-cent fine.

Once, while presenting at Holden Village, a remote retreat center in Western Washington, Gibbs complained about the "barbarians" who served only vegetarian meals at the facility, recalled William Diehl. Gibbs also objected to the center's rule that protected trails from overuse. He wanted to hike on any trail of his choosing, any day. But again, he didn't take himself too seriously. "The Holden staff distributed costumes for a Fourth of July parade," Diehl said. "Mark was given the costume and wig of King George in which he proudly strutted at the head of the parade."

When Gibbs was a guest at the Palo Alto home of Ted Carlstrom, who served as secretary of Vesper Society's board, Carlstrom's three teenage sons, who collected flags, would hang the Union Jack on their front door in Gibbs' honor. "It pleased him," Carlstrom said. The brilliance and charm of this remarkable character shone through during his visits. Carlstrom's recollections are worth citing at length:

> We all thoroughly enjoyed his visits with us. Mark prompted a conversation at the dinner table over a wide range of topics. He very definitely presided. He would seek viewpoints as he questioned the boys in the precise manner, we supposed, as might an English schoolmaster. He did it casually and enjoyably, yet effectively. He queried our sons about sports, literature, history, their studies and spoke of his travels. Those travels not only covered a broad range of places but the reason for his travel was always purposeful and constructive. Our sons were very interested in geography, and Mark was a walking atlas.
>
> On one occasion, after a visit, Mark sent our sons a letter. It was written in cipher … In Mark's introduction to his ciphered message, he challenged our sons to break the code so that they could read it. I'm not sure if the ciphered letter was prompted by Mark's conversation with our sons about secrecy, MI-5, codes and other Cold War topics. I suspect it was.
>
> A pleasant addition to our sons' interests was Mark's gifts to them of a number of editions of "Asterix" and "Tintin" illustrated stories or comic books published in Great Britain. He knew they would be fascinated with them. These books stimulated imagination in ways more constructive than U.S. comics. The books are still in our family library, now enjoyed by our grandchildren. Mark knew the stories, too.

Suffice it to say, Gibbs' personality was complex. "Mark had times of irritation and depression. That was part of Mark as was his ego," observed Robert Brorby. "But Mark was also charming, gracious, caring, and good company; he was a friend and a colleague, truly a remarkable person." Dynamism, contradictions, and a mixture of motivations marked his character. Like other Christians attempting to live out their callings, Gibbs revealed confidence and humility, frustration and exhilaration. He was angry at the church and in love with the church. He was worldly, and he was pious.

That piety, hidden by his stereotypical British reticence, revealed itself in his published prayers. Four pages of such prayers in an issue of the Audenshaw Papers include "A Prayer for those who are Uncertain": "O God, bless those who are not sure of things. ... Help them somehow to cling to the belief that a Father's hand will never cause His child a needless tear ... Amidst all the doubts and despairs and uncertainties, help us somehow still to be sure of You." At the end of his last book, *Christians With Secular Power* (1981), Gibbs shared Ten Prayers for Powerful Laity, one of which reads: "Lord, I do not ask for work equal to my strengths but for strength equal to your opportunities for me."

What held together all of his contradictions was a distinct understanding of Christian spirituality. In an essay published after his death in *Ministry Development Journal,* a U.S. Episcopal periodical, Gibbs described Christian spirituality as "keeping in touch with the divine and developing lifestyles in which we can serve God and our fellow citizens." The Christian life, he maintained, is a journey. "[W]e are a people on pilgrimage, citizens of the Kingdom, concerned more with the future than the past." Yet it is a journey through this world, so Christian spirituality must reckon with financial insecurities, health concerns, job pressures, and multiple demands on our time. It must "embrace our ordinary, banal, personal pains and perplexities" while also relating our private lives to the "ugly truths" of sickness, poverty and danger in the world. So Christian spirituality concerns the whole of life, with all of its complexity.

"Keeping in touch with the divine," or "walking with the Lord," could be expressed in a variety of ways, Gibbs said. He underscored the necessity of traditional Christian disciplines, such as prayer, reflection, worship and Bible study. However, he resisted the claim of any method to be "*the* one way to spiritual maturity." Instead, he placed the emphasis on grace: "The essential thing is to stress our fundamental Christian belief in the loving generosity of our God who is so anxious to bless us and use us ... A firm understanding of this ungrudging and loving eagerness to work through us is the first giant step towards a truly Christian spirituality."

The fact that Gibbs lived this credo made his impact on others very great. His strong voice, both actually and metaphorically, conveyed a sense of confidence and passion that revealed itself not only in his conversation but also in his writings. A 1980 essay, titled "Evangelism – The Awkward Subject," expressed his faith very concretely:

> The Christian faith is essentially a matter of commitment, yes, of a personal commitment, definite though maybe inarticulate. A personal response to the marvelous grace and generosity and love of God as shown in Jesus Christ. And for such a response, such a commitment, people have to be nudged, challenged, maybe kicked somehow into a thoughtful consideration of where they are spiritually. Without some such challenges in my own life, I do not believe I should have remained a practising Christian at all.

His Times

The concept of participating in the work of God in the world, crucial in Gibbs' life and in the activities of Vesper Society, was part of a larger ferment within Christianity in the decades following World War II. The trauma of the war as well as the church's ambivalent stance toward Nazism prompted Christians to rethink their mission, especially in Europe. At the same time, there was in the U.S. a ferment in the Christian world with a growth in church membership and an expansion of church-related agencies. It was an era of critique and construction. The role of the laity was re-asserted with its biblical and Reformational roots as the agents of change in all areas of society. This worldwide ferment in the late 1940s and 1950s no doubt influenced this energetic and very competent layman in Manchester.

The shift in the church's focus was particularly evident in Germany, where the church realized the necessity of engaging laypeople. The German church and the nation in general were painfully aware of the moral reconstruction needed to begin anew after the years of Nazi dominance. A horror had come upon the world, and the church was often complicit in its silence.

German Christians pursued this moral reconstruction through two movements that flourish still today. Both movements focused on the responsibility of laypeople to be active in seeking love and justice in the world. Gibbs participated in both organizations and later introduced Vesper Society to these like-minded groups.

The first was the Evangelical Academy movement initiated by Eberhard Müller in 1945 at Bad Boll near Stuttgart with some twenty conferences for the laity in its first year. One of Müller's early papers began: "The nearer the Hitler era came to its end, the more many members of the Confessing Church of Germany raised the question: 'What can we do to contribute to the rebuilding of government and society in the name of Christian responsibility?'" The academy was envisioned as an arena for exploration and reflection, what Müller called "a third location." Gibbs offered this definition: "They have been called 'academies' in the original, Platonic sense, since they are places for free discussion and argument." Ted Carlstrom further described the purpose of the academies:

The Protestant academies were founded after World War II as one of the commitments of the church to never again be compromised by a state as it had been by the National Socialists. Postwar, the church in each state in West Germany founded an academy to foster tolerant and open expressions of ideas about society, and provided a setting where ideas could be exchanged by conference participants without personal prejudice and in a context where the normative influence of Christian spiritual understandings could be heard.

Fifteen academies were established in Germany. The Reverend Paul-Gerhard Seiz, one of the directors of the Bad Boll academy who frequently worked with Gibbs on conferences at this institution, explained the academy's method:

The starting point is very often some everyday workplace experiences. We reflect together on these, and make some attempt to enable people to deal with the demands of daily routine. The next step is that, immediately, we try to relate such experiences to a wider political context ... It is in this context of political, professional, and personal experiences that we voice our fundamental theological convictions.

At the 40th anniversary of Bad Boll, West German President Richard von Weizächer said:

It is essential to build bridges of understanding, to invest time and effort to get real insights into the situation of people. But it is especially important to listen to those whose voices are usually ignored because their views might not be very popular at first sight. In this sense, I believe, academies are as necessary today as they were at the time when they were founded ... To listen to what are the essential questions in one's neighbour's life is something we often miss in our present society …

In 1981 Bad Boll had a staff of 180, of whom 55 were program staff, with about 450 conferences a year and about 15,000 participants. Vesper Society co-sponsored a number of conferences with various academies, and the Society's board of directors met at Bad Boll in 2004.

The second movement was the Kirchentag (literally, "church day"), sometimes translated as "church congress days." The gatherings occur approximately every two years in various German cities. Usually held for about five days, thousands of people, mostly Germans but also many others from around the world, enroll, in Gibbs' words, "for the whole programme of lectures, Bible studies, and discussion groups." He added: "It ends with a large open-air rally on the Sunday afternoon with anything up to 650,000 present …" This huge attendance at the final service in 1954 took place in Leipzig, which was still under the government of communist East Germany. And Gibbs was present at this momentous occasion.

The Kirchentag was begun by Reinold von Thadden-Trieglaff, a Pomeranian nobleman. Gibbs wrote a preface and epilogue as well as edited von Thadden-Trieglaff's biography, *A Man to Be Reckoned With*, in its English version in 1961. Originally written by Werner Huhne, Gibbs called it "the story of a great man and a great Christian." Since this individual significantly influenced Gibbs, it is important to understand his life and work.

From involvement in the international Student Christian Movement as a young man while attending a military academy, von Thadden-Trieglaff went on to serve in the army during World War I. During the 1930s he was active in the Confessing Church movement, which resisted Hitler's work to politicize the church for the Nazi cause. He was called up from the reserves in 1939 and became an officer in the Nazi army. The lieutenant spent most of his army service as regional commissioner in the university city of Louvain in Belgium. When the city celebrated the end of the war, the mayor, Dr. Richard Bruynoghe, world-famous bacteriologist professor at the university, expressed deep appreciation to von Thadden-Trieglaff for his work "in bringing the 80,000 citizens of Louvain more or less unscathed through the storms of war."

One incident typifies von Thadden-Trieglaff's ethic:

> Shortly before the end of the war, the officer in charge of the military police brought Thadden an order to shoot thirty hostages who had been held in the Louvain jail for a long time. Thadden asked the officer to give him a few moments to think. Then he sent for him again and told him he would not carry out the order. His honor as an officer and a nobleman would not allow him to execute innocent people who had nothing to do with the sabotage incident. The officer said nothing and did nothing. The hostages were not executed.

A few years after the war, a young officer asked von Thadden-Trieglaff how he could have worn the uniform of Hitler's army even for a single day. He answered:

> There is not one of us whose actions as a soldier in the war were always completely logical. If we, if I, had always acted logically, we should have ended upon the scaffold as conscientious objectors in the first months of the war. I had no special formula as a German officer in Hitler's army beyond a keen sense of responsibility in each actual situation and a continued realization day by day of the power of the forgiveness of God. You are right in saying there is no war without guilt, but there is also the truth of the Gospel that there are plenty of opportunities for the Christian in an evil world to live by faith, and to affirm his obedience to the Will of God *in each new actual decision he is called upon to take.*

Later, von Thadden-Trieglaff was wounded during an air raid and went back to the family estate in Pomerania. When the Russian army arrived, they took him as a prisoner "somewhere in the marshes between the spurs of the Urals and the Arctic." When he was finally released in late 1945, he was a half-starved skeleton of a man who once weighed 180 pounds and now weighed scarcely 90.

While he recovered, his former friends from the Student Christian Movement persuaded him to pursue his vision of a huge gathering of German laity who would wrestle with crucial ethical and moral issues facing the nation. With only one staff person and a timeline of two years, this improbable man did the impossible: rallying 25,000 participants and 200,000 worshipers in the final service at Essen for the first Kirchentag in 1950.

Gibbs clearly held von Thadden-Trieglaff in high esteem and saw him as a mentor. Here was a member of the laity who lived his faith amid impossibly difficult situations and had caught the vision of what laity needed: education and encouragement to live the faith within secular structures, no matter what they be. In 1958 this German leader wrote:

> The Kirchentag has set itself the task to call Protestant lay Christians to their responsibilities in all sectors of public life and to make them active, particularly in the economic, social and political fields where Christian principles are on trial and where Christian obedience has to stand the test. The layman is anything but some sort of marginal figure on the outskirts of the Church. He is the essential interpreter of the Christian message in the battlefield of the world. Therefore he must be spiritually prepared for open confession of his faith, and for active service in everyday life as well as in the congregation.

Such a ringing challenge became the credo and mandate for all of Gibbs' work. Clearly, the Kirchentag was close to Gibbs' heart as he wrote in 1978:

> Yes, the Kirchentag is very open, and very varied; and
> you will not find neat, packaged 'Christian answers' to
> everything. But it is much more than any liberal debat-
> ing forum. Such openness and such variety is offered for
> *theological reasons*, because the leaders of the Kirchentag
> believe that we must search this hard to see what God
> is saying to us today, both from the Bible and from
> Christian tradition and also from all kinds of human
> ideas outside the institutional churches ... There is a
> constant demand that the participants consider again
> the fundamental questions of human existence and the
> deepest questions of our Christian faith. Perhaps the
> only sin at a Kirchentag is to remain apathetic.

Gibbs served in the important post of chair of the International
Committee of the Kirchentag from 1958 to 1978.

The Kirchentag, academies and other laity initiatives fed a hunger
for theological reflection in the post-war years. Many writings on the
ministry of the laity were published during this time and would have
been familiar to a voracious reader such as Gibbs. Earlier, Anglican
Archbishop William Temple issued an important work, *Christianity
and the Social Order* (1942). *Church and People in an Industrial City*
(1958), written by British clergyman Ted Wickham, related the Gospel message to urban life in Sheffield and inspired many, including Gibbs
and Morton. A spate of other books appeared in

A scene from the 1967 Kirchentag at Hannover,
Germany. [Photo courtesy of the German
Protestant Kirchentag]

the 1950s from many different Christian traditions such as: *The Company of the Committed* (1951), by the American Quaker Elton Trueblood; *Lay People in the Church* (1957), by the French Dominican Yves Congar; and *A Theology of the Laity* (1959), by the Dutch Reformed theologian Hendrik Kraemer. Each of these books challenged laypeople to be salt and leaven in the world.

And laypeople rallied to the call. Vesper Society co-founder Bob Cummings, for instance, accepted an invitation from Dr. James P. Beasom Jr., president of the Pacific Southwest Synod of the Lutheran Church in America, to help recruit lay leaders in the 1950s. Beasom proposed a new program, The Committee of 1,000, which would raise awareness of the work of laypeople through local meetings and large gatherings. He needed the help of Cummings, who was then a partner in California Tank & Manufacturing Company. Cummings' business partners were active church leaders in the Pentecostal tradition, so they supported his involvement in the laity movement. Piggybacking on business trips, Cummings would speak to groups of lay leaders eager to integrate their faith and work. The Committee of 1,000 helped establish congregational chapters of the Lutheran Brotherhood, a fraternal benefit society known today as Thrivent Financial for Lutherans, and that initiative fueled conversations and area meetings of lay leaders. "I found a lot of men in the West who had the same feelings and the same desire," Cummings said.

Meanwhile, some international church bodies also affirmed the ministry of the laity. In 1948 the World Council of Churches was formed and at its first assembly in a report on the laity stated that "the Lord Jesus claims the whole of life, and therefore, the Christian faith necessarily demands expression in all realms of life." In the Evanston Assembly in 1954, the Council set forth this often-repeated declaration:

> The time has come to make the ministry of the laity
> explicit, visible and active in the world. The real battles

of the faith today are being fought in factories, shops, offices, and farms, in political parties and government agencies, in countless homes, in the press, radio and television, in the relationship of nations. Very often it is said that the church should 'go into these spheres'; but the fact is, that the church is already in these spheres in the persons of its laity.

One of the World Council's first presidents, Joseph Oldham, amplified this new tone. As noted earlier, Oldham had formed in 1942 the Christian Frontier Council, which was described by Gibbs in *Christians With Secular Power*: "[T]he term *frontier* ... does not refer to some kind of barrier or no man's land *between* church people and secular experts. It has reference to the new frontiers of human knowledge and experience which God calls church people and others to explore *together*." Gibbs later served on this council. Its purpose, articulated by Oldham, encapsulated Gibbs' own mission:

> If Christianity is not something existing apart from life, but the transfiguration of life itself – and that means in the end the transfiguration of the whole of life – it is to those who are on the frontline of the battle and are exposed to the severest tests who are best able to teach us what Christianity means as a living faith.

Another friend and mentor of Gibbs, Hans-Ruedi Weber (*The Layman in Christian History*, 1963), as the secretary of the Department of the Laity of the World Council of Churches (1955-1961), provided strong leadership to the movement, as reflected in the 1961 World Council Assembly in New Delhi whose message included: "The real letter to the world today does not consist of words. We Christian people, wherever we are, are a letter from Christ to the world." A later image in this message was even more powerful:

> Christ the light did not remain outside the world to

illuminate it from above, but entered into human life, conquered the darkness and radiates light from within. This says to us that wherever we are in the world, God is there before us — the light is already there. The responsibility of the laity is to serve as reflecting mirrors or focusing lenses, to beam the light into all parts of the life of the world.

In *The New Reformation*, published in 1965, the year Vesper Society was founded, Bishop J.A.T. Robinson pointed out that the resource for theology, in contrast to previous eras when episcopal, monastic, or pastoral theology provided the starting point, was now the people of God in the world.

These four simple words, "the people of God," reverberated throughout Christendom in the mid-1960s when Vatican II declared that all who are baptized are the people of God, the holy priesthood (I Peter 2), and all of humankind is called to become the people of God. The Vatican Council employed familiar biblical images concerning the laity: "The laity is called in particular to make the church present and effective in those places and circumstances where only through them can she become the salt of the earth"; and later, "They are called there by God so that by exercising their proper function and being led by the spirit of the gospel they can work for the sanctification of the world from within, in the manner of leaven."

The theological reflection was provocative and inspiring. The postwar era of critique and construction, ideas and action, galvanized reflective and enterprising Christian leaders. Amid this ferment, it was almost inevitable that Gibbs and Vesper Society's founders would find one another.

2

Sharing a Vision

Building Relationships

The initial connection between Gibbs and Vesper Society, described in the Introduction, was the result of a triple play: from Weihe to Spindt to Heckathorn.

All three people were very active in the United Lutheran Church in America at the congregational, synodical, and national levels. The president of the Pacific Southwest Synod, Dr. James P. Beasom Jr., was instrumental in connecting these three men to one another, to Bob Cummings and, later, to Robert Brorby.

Spindt, Heckathorn, Cummings, and Brorby were all pivotal in the early history of the Society and its relationship to Gibbs. In strange and providential ways, through planned as well as serendipitous encounters, through geographic proximity (all lived in the Bay Area) and travel to Europe, they formed a bond of friendship and sharing of gifts. Little did they know that all of this would lead to the impressive history of Vesper Society as well as to its sponsorship of Gibbs, who greatly influenced the movement of the ministry of the laity in the U.S. and throughout the world.

As noted earlier, Clifton Weihe invited Gibbs to Messiah Lutheran Church in Redwood City to lead a week of seminars on "The Laity and Education." The meetings were well attended. Held in cooperation with a local community college, the seminars drew faculty and students as well as townspeople and representatives from Stanford University. In November 1969, Messiah invited Gibbs to lead another seminar for laypeople and clergy on the theme of "The Laity: Education and Ministry." The Sunday event was to conclude with an evening service with "Gibbs in the pulpit," according to a letter of Weihe, who was then the church's associate pastor.

Various seminars in the Bay Area followed, providing material for Gibbs and Morton's second book, *God's Lively People*, published in 1971. Prior to coming to this congregation, Weihe had been a staff member of the Board of Social Missions of the United Lutheran Church in America and a leader in laity circles. In between his two positions, he spent considerable time in Europe to learn more about the German Evangelical Academies. While on his travels, he was introduced to Gibbs.

As noted in the Introduction, George Spindt was the senior pastor of Messiah Lutheran Church at the time; he had been vice president of the Pacific Southwest Synod and, as noted earlier, had served the Lutheran World Federation in its work with refugees in Europe after the war. In 1974 Spindt became CEO of Vesper Society.

Eugene Heckathorn, member of the synod's executive committee and one of the founders of the Society, was a dynamic businessman who owned his own company at age 29. Heckathorn had met Cummings outside the 1964 Lutheran Church convention in Harrisburg, Pennsylvania. "Are you out here boondoggling?" Heckathorn asked Cummings. Their friendship blossomed immediately. "Gene was a layman whose horizon of life's opportunities and responsibilities was boundless," Cummings once said. "Working with him had the challenge of racing with a giant – never being able to catch up – but always assured that the contest was most worthy."

Heckathorn and Spindt had many "deep ethical conversations"

about Heckathorn's "crisis of conscience," according to Spindt. Heckathorn was extremely concerned about the use of pesticides on California fields as well as the use of napalm in the Vietnam War. His company, United-Heckathorn, had produced both products. Heckathorn had been at Harvard earning his MBA at the same time as Robert McNamara, who later served as Secretary of Defense during the Vietnam War. These two men continued to have some contact with one another. Thus amid Heckathorn's ethical dilemmas about his company's production of destructive substances, he also dedicated great energy toward launching an organization whose very essence was to contribute to the good of humankind. Like many of us, he wrestled with how his faith related to the complexity of his life.

Heckathorn recognized that the new Society needed to enlarge its vision. So he enlisted Spindt to travel to Europe on behalf of the Society. According to the organization's minutes of May 23, 1969, "A resolution was approved sending George Spindt to Geneva, Switzerland 'for the purpose of developing more international aspects for Vesper Society.'" Gibbs helped Spindt make contacts abroad. At the next meeting of the Society on June 27, 1969, the minutes state, "Pastor Spindt reported on plans for his trip to London and Geneva to promote studies for Vesper Society," and also "Mr. Mark Gibbs of the Church of England and the World Council of Churches reported on possible areas in which Vesper Society could be useful in the rest of the world."

At Spindt's suggestion, Heckathorn agreed to meet Gibbs in May 1970, since, according to Spindt, both were struggling with how Christians were to live their faith in the world. Gibbs wrote two accounts of this courtship years later, the one in 1980 already provided in the Introduction, the second in 1985, which includes further details of this crucial meeting:

> I remember dear George Spindt's efforts to get me involved in Vesper Society. I remember one or two sem-

inars we had in Redwood City when he was at Messiah Church, and when Cliff Weihe was the associate there. I remember meeting him from time to time when I came to the city, for of course I came here long before I knew about Vesper Society.

I remember the first serious conversation I had with Gene Heckathorn. I had to go to Portland, Oregon, because he had not been well, and I had there one of the most extraordinary evenings of my life. We had some quite good food and drink; and then he talked, and he lectured, and he brainwashed me, and he indoctrinated me, and he drowned me in a kind of exuberant vision of what Vesper Society was going to do. It was a vision of a renewed church in America, and a vision of Vesper Society as the instrument for this renewal. And of course, he gave me my instructions. I was to drop everything and join this great movement. I was in particular to produce and edit a great glossy magazine for the Society, which would give prestige to Vesper and wisdom to the nation. As far as I could see a kind of mixture of *Foreign Affairs Quarterly* and *Fortune* magazine. And this went on until 1:00 in the morning.

I didn't say very much, partly because I didn't want to, and partly because I didn't have a chance anyway. But I didn't go to bed straight away, I thought very hard and reflected; and the next morning I said one or two things to him at breakfast, and I repeated them in a letter from British Columbia a day or two later. And I said: No, I can't abandon all my work with Audenshaw and in Europe. I had already been for five years the Director of the Audenshaw Foundation, and I wasn't about to give all of that up. No, I said. And he didn't like this very much. Also I said: No, I will not produce yet another glossy magazine, I think it would be a waste of a great

deal of money. There are already a lot of expensive magazines going into the trash cans of busy executives. But
then I said: Yes, I will ask my trustees if I may edit a
packet of good material taken from the magazines
which already exist, and, yes, I shall be honored if I can
advise you about your seminars and your laity programs.

Otto Bremer, a Lutheran pastor who later was a key figure in the
Society, especially in the relationship of business and ethics, recalled
this meeting in a tribute at Gibbs' death:

Mark himself admits when he first met with the late
Gene Heckathorn, he wasn't convinced there would be
any kind of relationship with the Vesper Society. This
was so even though a good friend, George Spindt, urged
him to meet Gene ... Mark managed to slip in a few
questions that evening but was really more over-
whelmed with his dynamic and determined dinner
companion. For those who know Gene, you know full
well what Mark was feeling. That was Gene – he could
make you dizzy when he talked about his dreams ... he
was hard to say no to.

Gibbs and Heckathorn both possessed a passion for the laity's vocation
in the world. According to Brorby, "Gene would have been attracted to
Mark as the leading 'theologian of the laity' and gadfly among the
national and international laity of many denominations."

About a week after the meeting, Gibbs spelled out his understanding of his assignment in a letter to Heckathorn:

1. You want me to make further contacts with the
World Council of Churches and other agencies and try
to find several places overseas – preferably not too far
from one another – where (a) managerial advice and/or
(b) professional advice from competent Christian laymen would be really welcome.

2. You want me to help design and be a major resource for one or two new style "retreats" for Vesper people and similar laity, the first being 13-14 November.

3. You would like me to help with and be co-editor of a regular "mailing" of suitable articles of professional, theological and ethical interest.

Later in the letter, Gibbs indicated their common complaint: "... I shall be very glad to work with some people who can avoid some of the churchy 'micky[sic] mouse' style we have both suffered from so often."

Gibbs concluded the correspondence with a typical revelation of his modesty and thrift: "For the time being, I will ask my Treasurer to claim at the rate of $50 a day when I am really engaged on Vesper business; but of course this will not mean that I only open your files once or twice a month. Let me know if you think we are at any time claiming too much; but I don't think you will find we are at all extravagant in the way we work."

With that understatement, the connection between Gibbs and Vesper Society was forged. Providence, we might say, was at work. "Mark Gibbs – and this I can only speculate about, but believe – must have been elated to discover Vesper Society," said Carlstrom. "Mark's sympathy of interest with people associated with Vesper Society may even have been regarded as pre-ordained rather than coincidental although that may be a bit dangerous to say." A common passion formed the basis of the relationship. "Shared was a desire to advocate a modern expression of vocation of the laity that was *not dependent upon an ecclesial structure* but built on a framework of individual faith and personal skill and competence," said Carlstrom [emphasis added]. "In Vesper Society, Mark truly had found a patron (in the best sense of the term) and occasional partner."

Gibbs was not a staff member of the Society, but a contractual relationship ensued in which the Society underwrote much of Gibbs' salary and expenses for his work in the U.S. and abroad. Gibbs continued his major work with the Audenshaw Foundation. Gibbs was drawn to Vesper Society, in part, because he could travel around North America and elsewhere at the Society's expense – "a cost Audenshaw could ill afford" when Gibbs was spending much time on Society work, noted Brorby. "This was one of the reasons why, at times, Mark would get so mad at Vesper – he felt that Vesper was not paying Audenshaw enough money for the use of his time, which he saw as unfair to Audenshaw, his first love."

And yet the relationship, loose and sometimes frustrating to both parties, nevertheless continued for sixteen years. One of the major reasons was that Gibbs, as a scholar-teacher-practitioner, revealed in his writings and his work a vision that resonated with the mission of the Society.

Education for the World

Clearly, Gibbs and Vesper Society had much in common. Both believed that Christian faith must be lived out in the world, embodied in the work of peace and justice. What Gibbs provided was a framework, as Brorby has said, "of the inclusion of ethical and moral perspectives in the consideration of socio-economic-political discussions sponsored by Vesper …" Thus Gibbs' thinking and the Society's activities converged at several important points. As Cummings recently stated in an interview:

> Mark gave his life to the program of convincing the church that they have to make it possible for the laity to serve their church like they preached they'd like to have them serve. So we joined Mark in that and had Mark come on board with us so that we could get the church to provide the opportunities for laity to express their faith, and that's how we got going in these issues.

But convincing the church to welcome the ministry of the laity in the world was a struggle. The church was more than happy to put laypeople to work inside the church, Gibbs noted, but the institution ignored the more important task of supporting laity in the world. Cummings said this reality was a source of ongoing conflict: "[W]e were always fighting, not fighting, we were always working to have the church open its doors in ways that only laypeople can fill them and to get the satisfaction of serving the church in meaningful ways." Yet when the church did display openness, the result was, in Cummings' words, "fulfillment":

> The church opened up the opportunities for us as laypeople to serve the church as we had asked to serve, and it was a fulfillment of our desire … Gene and I often spoke of that fulfillment. Mark Gibbs appreciated it, too, because we used Mark many times … and Mark was bringing opportunities to us, too. It was the same kind of fulfillment for Mark as it was for us.

Cummings and Heckathorn's undertaking to rescue struggling Lutheran institutions would have captured Gibbs' attention, since the management needs of these institutions confirmed Gibbs' critique that the church generally did not have adequate knowledge of business or economics. Surely Gibbs would have been delighted, and perhaps surprised, that Franklin Clark Fry, the leader of the Lutheran Church in America at that time, had turned to two people with the skills and faith commitment to address the situation. Cummings and Heckathorn, to use the title of Gibbs' later book, were *Christians With Secular Power*. The opening page of this book begins with a collect that might well have been prayed about these two men: "Grant that they may both perceive and know what things they ought to do, and also may have grace and power faithfully to fulfill the same."

There was no doubt that Gibbs and the founders of Vesper Society understood where their work needed to begin. "Our First Priority," as noted earlier, is what Gibbs called this common focus in the premier edition of *Vesper Exchange*:

> In fact the main vocation of God's people is not to build and to support church structures (though some of these may certainly be necessary). It is to find a new style of humanity -- in explicitly Christian terms to be the Body of Christ, the intelligent and committed embodiment of Christian love and service – *in the secular structures in which God has placed or will place them.*

Embedded in this profound credo are two central themes: first, the call to be part of the new humanity in Christ, and second, the call to work in the secular structures. Gibbs reiterated these two principles in a 1984 essay: "Our vocation – the vocation of all human beings – is the call from God to be part of the new humanity in Jesus Christ, to be citizens of the Kingdom and the People of God. And this is true for all of us, whatever our occupation and job and indeed whether we are employed or not." These beliefs were made concrete in a joint paper of Heckathorn and Gibbs titled "The Development of Large-Scale Corporate Caring," which they prepared as a "position paper" for the planning of the 1973 German Kirchentag in Düsseldorf. Two sentences convey the texture of the paper:

> There are also, perhaps particularly in North America, many "progressive" religious people who nevertheless will only consider "loving deeply" those whom they know face-to-face – and who will not face the problems of achieving justice and fair health and educational structures for those whom they will never meet personally. ...
>
> We are called by God to seek both a deep love for those we know personally, and also real justice for very many people we shall never know at all.

To promote love and justice in the world, Christians must first understand the world's structures, Gibbs and the Society maintained. To do this, Christians must listen carefully to people in these institutions. *Vesper Exchange* was one vehicle to promote such understanding. The publication's purpose, as Gibbs put it in his opening editorial, was "first, to challenge those who work within the structures of political and industrial and economic life to see where they are, and what these structures are doing, for good or ill, to them and other people. And second, to offer some material which may genuinely help them work out their responsible vocations." He himself set the tone by articles such as "Economic Ignorance Is Very Dangerous" and "Civil Rights Are Not Expendable." The scope of his writing ranged widely but always with an ethical framework: "The Christian Intellectual," "Travelmania Trap," "Intelligent Economics," and "The Vocation of Technologists." And he reprinted writers from diverse backgrounds, among them, historian David Halberstam, foreign-policy expert George Kennan, musician Yehudi Menuhin, and TV journalist Edwin Newman. George Spindt recently described the format of the publication:

> Gene [Heckathorn] wanted him to edit a kind of slick magazine on all the things we were doing. Mark had a different idea and developed what was called *Vesper Exchange*. It looks like a kind of a half-baked-put-together thing, with loose papers and so on, but it was very purposefully done that way. The idea was that busy people on a commuter train could take his paper out, put it in their coat pocket and read it, and if they wanted, mark it up or tear it up or whatever.

Gibbs offered his own assessment of the publication: "I believe that over the months, our different issues ... have helped readers to see more clearly the sharp and yet very complicated issues which disturb the modern world."

Gibbs' editorial leadership was dominant, according to Carlstrom. Editorial board members "had little to do with editing or publishing other than perhaps the suggestion of an article, or an occasional review of an already published article which Mark sent over for comment on its suitability for reprint in a forthcoming edition," Carlstrom said. Gibbs kept a very close hold on all aspects of *Vesper Exchange* while Vesper Society underwrote the costs. Gibbs desired in the 1970s that *Vesper Exchange* be more fully supported, yet Gibbs wanted that support according to his terms, Carlstrom recalled:

> As I understood Mark's request, he wanted me to think about how additional support for *Vesper Exchange* could take place and that I should put it however I wished to the board of directors of Vesper Society. My suggestion, stated to the board with Mark present, was that it affirm *Vesper Exchange* as a publication of Vesper Society and that it make the editorial board truly function as an internal board capable of drumming up some significant charitable contributions for the publication's support. I also suggested that Vesper Society and Mark plan on reinforcing Mark's work so that there would be continuation of the publication as a house effort so that in the event of Mark's disability, retirement or death, the publication could continue. Mark didn't wait for the idea to be discussed by the board. He tersely interjected by stating he did not want an editorial or publications board that would meet or conduct itself as such and that he did not want fund-raising appeals for the effort. And while it was plain that he would accept more financial support from the Vesper Society for the publication, any suggestion about organizing its production in a way that would perpetuate it was not welcome. He said, flat out, that when he died, *Vesper Exchange* would, and should, die with him. I withdrew my suggestion.

Vesper Exchange, which continued until 1982 when Gibbs' health declined, was thus one route toward a larger objective for Gibbs and the Society: to educate and support Christians in their secular vocations. Without such support, Christians would tend to separate Sunday from Monday. Gibbs and the Society pushed for something more. Thus in 1977, Gibbs proposed another publication, similar in format to the earlier effort, to be called *Laity Exchange*. It was to be aimed specifically at supporting the laity movement, both individuals and organization. Again, he specified that the format would be "modest" – offset printed, in a mailing or filing envelope – "but not sloppy." The Society once more provided production assistance and financial support beyond what Gibbs was able to raise through modest subscription fees. Usually published quarterly, twenty-eight issues appeared under Gibbs' editorship.

A memo from Gibbs prior to the first issue accurately described the contents of the future publication:

a. Reports of the laity centres and educational experiments

b. "Think Pieces" about the development of laity education

c. The Audenshaw Book Suggestion Sheets and other notes about materials

d. Short notes about all kinds of developments in the field of the laity

He added another proviso, which was also followed: "I would hope that it will be both ecumenical and international ..." Published in collaboration with the Audenshaw Foundation, *Laity Exchange* was sponsored by formal and informal church organizations in the U.S., Canada and Britain, including the National Council of Churches, the British Council of Churches, most of the major denominations, and a number of international bodies such as the Lutheran World Federation and the

World Association for Christian Communication. In 1985 Gibbs reported that "*Laity Exchange* has 60 sponsors, 70 correspondents. Goes to a wide variety of Third World libraries, and this is expanding rapidly." After Gibb's death in 1986, George Spindt edited three issues of *Laity Exchange*, the first being a selection of a dozen articles of what Gibbs called Laity Basics. Nelvin Vos edited six more issues, and Vesper Society published three more until ending the publication in 1992.

Gibbs and the Society took the educational initiative further with the launching of a lecture series. Beginning in 1981, the Vesper/Audenshaw Laity Lecture (later called the Mark Gibbs Memorial Lecture) featured outstanding public figures speaking on major social issues. Gibbs himself set the tone in the inaugural lecture, "The Development of a Strong and Committed Laity": "We need laity who are able to handle questions of belief and skepticism, and questions which criticize both society and church. And laity who are able to handle questions of ambiguity and compromise (by which the world is run)."

The succeeding speakers came from a wide variety of religious and social backgrounds: Roman Catholic lay leaders such as Abigail McCarthy ("Women as Laity," 1982) and Dolores Leckey ("The Laity's Prophetic Questions: Challenge and Hope for the Church," 1985); Baptist theologian George Peck, president of Andover Newton Theological Seminary ("Christ's Whole Body in Ministry: Recovering a Central Biblical Image," 1983); Lutheran journalist Charles Austin ("Christians With Media Power," 1984); Evangelical leader Richard Mouw, president of Fuller Theological Seminary ("Gaining Strength— The Long-Term Prospects for the American Laity," 1986); Pauline Webb from the BBC ("The Media as a Frontline Mission," 1987); Lutheran businessman William Diehl ("Confronting Dualism," 1989); noted author and sociologist Robert Bellah ("Discipleship and Citizenship in the Workplace," 1990); Senator Paul Simon ("Conflicts of Religion in Politics," 1991); civil rights leader Rosa Parks ("A Look at America: Past, Present and Future," 1992); and two African-American Baptist laymen from Oakland, California, lawyer John Harrison Jr. and physician Robert Scott III ("Making a Difference: Challenge and Hope in the Here and Now," 1994). The last lecture was presented in 1995 at Hartford Seminary in Connecticut by Bernice Johnson Reagon, Curator Emeritus of the National Museum of American History. The lectures usually had two settings, one in the Bay Area and a second elsewhere in the U.S., such as Chicago or Boston. Several presentations were later published and distributed widely.

Vesper Society's support of all these activities, including Gibbs' work, testified to the Society's commitment to laity education. Through the 1980s, the Society was regarded as a primary convener of laypeople who were eager to explore their role in the world.

By 1985 Gibbs had a broad vision of his work on behalf of Vesper Society. A memo with a seven-point long-range plan, titled "The Vesper/Audenshaw Laity Information Program," included not only all of the above activities but also cited a new avenue of education already underway: a series of Laity Exchange Books published by Fortress Press and edited by Gibbs. He laid out the purpose of the series in his introduction to the first volume, *Called to Holy Worldliness* by Richard Mouw (1980):

> Here is the first of a new series of Laity Exchange Books, which are specifically designed to help Christian people, both laity and clergy, to think further about the calling and the responsibilities of the laity today. We shall concentrate particularly on the life and witness of lay people in the world, in their work and politics and leisure.

By 1985, four volumes in addition to Mouw's work had been published: *Christians With Secular Power* (1981), by Gibbs himself and dedicated "To My Friends and Colleagues at Vesper Society"; *Thank God, It's Monday!* (1982), by William Diehl; *Christian Maturity and Christian*

Success (1982), by British theologian Daniel Jenkins; and *Seven Days A Week: Faith in Action* (1985), by Nelvin Vos. Three more volumes were projected, but with Gibbs' death in 1986, only one was published, *All God's People Are Ministers* (1993), by American theologian Patricia Page and edited by Nelvin Vos.

For Gibbs and Vesper Society, the vision was not only local and national but also international. "Today San Leandro, tomorrow the world," the Society's leaders often joked, but the comment captured the breadth of their interests. Moreover, the widening of their vision reflected their era, as political, social and religious changes collapsed global distances and called for new social engagement by Christian leaders. Some of these changes will be explored more fully in Chapter 4, but here we note how the vision broadened to match the scope of Gibbs' and the Society's calling and their ambition.

Gibbs helped expand the Society's horizons by facilitating global contacts. Immediately upon Gibbs' involvement with the Society, he encouraged George Spindt to attend the German Kirchentag. As chairman of the International Committee of the Kirchentag from 1958 to 1978, Gibbs was the midwife for the ongoing participation of the Society in this powerful event. The Kirchentag attracted many Society leaders, including Robert Brorby, who served in the 1970s as the Society's representative on the event's International Committee.

Gibbs also cultivated a relationship between the Society and the German Evangelical Academies. Especially meaningful were the pre-Kirchentag conferences held at the academy centers in which participants from the Society met with European leaders to discuss significant issues. Typical of these conferences was the 1981 consultation at Bad Boll, which addressed German concerns about U.S. unilateralism that was feared from the newly elected Reagan administration. According to Ted Carlstrom, who participated in the sessions, an assistant secretary of defense had recently attended the annual NATO

defense ministers' conference in Munich and had unsettled German
leaders by saying that while "détente" with the USSR might be West
German policy, it wouldn't work for the U.S. Carlstrom described
Gibbs' important role in the undertaking:

> Mark had a large number of German friends and con-
> tacts. His encouragement to the academy had brought
> an impressive array of very knowledgeable Germans to
> speak with a group from the U.S. who didn't have the
> competence in foreign affairs topics that the Germans
> had. ... Mark shared an introduction and later a sum-
> mary of the conference with academy director Gunther
> Metzger in a very impressive way. Together they set the
> tone of the dialogue by the disparate group. It was
> superbly done.

During the conference another group, which included a number of
German émigrés from Silesia, was also meeting at the academy.
Carlstrom overheard Gibbs addressing this group in German: "Mark's
language skills, far from being meager as he so modestly had said, were
fluent and spoken without hesitation ... We thus saw another side of
Mark Gibbs, one which left us again impressed ..."

Following this event, Carlstrom was concerned that persons from
the U.S. had come to Bad Boll with a good deal of interest but were
utterly unequipped to discuss the issues of international security and
peace with the level of competence of the German delegation. Thus
he along with Gibbs, Spindt, and Paul-Gerhard Seiz, Bad Boll's former director, began to plan an ambitious interchange to be called
"Wege zum Freiden," or Roads to Peace. Carlstrom recently recalled
the undertaking:

> We came to the conclusion that we should have a series
> of three English-speaking conferences over about an
> 18-month span on peace and security issues in German-

American relations. It was to be carried on as a joint program of Vesper Society and the Leiterkreis [leadership circle, that is, the directors] of the Evangelische Akademiem in Deutschland.

The first conference was held in June 1982 at Bad Boll: "Preventing Nuclear War." The second took place in January 1983 at Menlo Park, California: "National Security, National Interest: Economic and Social Justice Aspects." That original series ended in June 1983 at the academy in Loccum, Germany, with a conference on "Confidence-Building Measures and Global Security," while subsequent conversations took up the theme of peace in Central America.

A Russian Orthodox cleric, his translator, and Mark Gibbs follow the proceedings in the June 1983 "Roads to Peace" conference at the Evangelical Academy at Loccum, Germany. [Photo by Lee Langan]

Participants included Arthur Burns, former U.S. ambassador to Germany; Maj. General Richard Bowman, who served on the Pentagon staff of Caspar Weinberger; Jewjenii Grigoriev, editor for Pravda; and Philip Farley, retired director of the U.S. Arms Control and Disarmament Agency. The Bad Boll session included former U.S. Ambassador for Arms Control Jonathan Dean, who had represented the U.S. at the NATO-Warsaw Pact force reduction negotiations in Vienna from 1973-1981. Among the Germans were East and West German military officers, clergy, educators, bankers and lawyers. Some thirty-five Germans participated in the U.S. session.

Carlstrom summarized Gibbs' part in the project:

> At each of the conferences Mark served as one of the session chairs. And at the conclusion of each of the conferences, both sides of the joint committee met. At

these, Mark offered useful comments. He had been to
enough conferences around the world to know whereof
he spoke … Whether Mark fully appreciated it or not,
his example and his encouragement was the source and
impetus of this entire effort. That's influence.

Earlier conferences preceding this series focused on laity topics,
such as the 1977 consultation at Bad Boll on "Trends and Priorities
Today in Laity Work" in which Gibbs, Spindt, Brorby and some thirty
other American and German leaders participated. The 1978 conference
featured presentations such as "Supporting the Laity in their Mission in
the World" by Gibbs, "The Mission of the American Laity" by Richard
Mouw, and "Lay People in the Urban Setting" by Will Herzfeld,
African-American pastor of Bethlehem Lutheran Church in Oakland
who later became president of
the Association of Evangelical
Lutheran Churches, one of
the predecessor bodies of the
ELCA.

The U.S. side of the "Roads to Peace" program
committee confers at Loccum, Germany, in
June 1983: (from left) Mark Gibbs, Otto
Bremer, Bruce Johnson, Al Rudisill, and Ted
Carlstrom. [Photo by Lee Langan]

Clearly, these experiences
broadened the horizons of the
Society's leaders. "This was an
era in which Vesper was active
in involving laity with the
power to effect change in
issues of war and peace to actually do that – an activity of a small nonprofit group to affect or help others to affect public policy," said Brorby.
Gibbs' worldwide contacts stimulated the Society's international work
and profoundly shaped the organization's future. "It was a heady time,"
added Spindt.

⊛ 3 ⊛

'Deep Convictions and Hard Thinking'

Gibbs' Themes

In the title of a 1982 *Laity Exchange* article, Gibbs affirmed that "Yes, We Must Be a Peculiar People," which he described as "a matter of working politically and structurally about *justice* for the 'outsiders'…" Working for the "outsiders" would naturally lead Christian laypeople beyond the parish, to the outside world. Hence, Gibbs' emphasis on the location of Christian love and service: the vocation of God's people is to be the body of Christ "*in the secular structures in which God has placed or will place them.*" Gibbs and Morton in *God's Lively People* made clear that the use of the term "secular" is not one of condemnation but one that "recalls us to the truth, which is asserted in the Bible from beginning to end, *that it is only in this world that we can know God and that it is only in the contemporary world that we can serve him.*"

Gibbs and Morton noted that it was not until the 20th century that "secular" picked up its negative connotation, namely that "man was self-sufficient and had no need of the hypothesis of God." They wanted to draw out the older meaning: secular as temporal, "belonging to time." "[W]e have to recover the true use of the word, to assert the belief that time, as well as space, is God's creation and where we know him," they wrote. We cannot overemphasize the importance of this belief for Gibbs. He and Morton added,

> [B]ecause the word "religious" still has a meaning for us, Christians sometimes talk as if there were two worlds opposed to each other, and they lived in them both and could choose which to serve. Indeed, they often talk as if there were a lot of worlds to which they belonged and they could jump from one to the other – the political world, the academic world, the world of sport, the world of the Church. But the word "secular" will tolerate no such division, any more than the word "Christian" will. Men know only one world, as they know only one life. We can give it whatever name we like but we cannot divide it.

This theme, that there is one world and that it is the calling of God's people to "find a new style of humanity" here, was Gibbs' "First Priority."

A second theme was the absolute necessity of Christians bringing the ethical and moral perspectives of their faith to bear in the spheres of socio-economic-political discussions and action. Careful discernment is a prerequisite in order to work within the complexities of secular society. When laity are immersed in the complex work of love and justice in their daily lives, Gibbs wrote in a letter to a World Council of Churches official, they encounter constant challenges: "[There are] ambiguities and responsible compromises laypeople must accept and wrestle with day by day. Of course it is right to expect a bold and prophetic witness, but problems in Monday's world are rarely good against evil, light against darkness. So many decisions are concerned with different shades of grey."

If, as we have seen, Gibbs challenged Christians to be engaged in the structures of the world and to relate their Christian faith within those structures, then Christians need to be competent, hardheaded realists, another motif in Gibbs' writings. Already in *God's Lively People*, Gibbs and Morton were explicit on the importance of careful thought within the life of Christians: "The true people of God are those who are as prepared to think with honesty as they are to act with enthusiasm ... The challenge to God's people is to live and think."

Gibbs called for "a matching of deep convictions and hard thinking." One of his major subheadings in the first Vesper/Audenshaw Laity Lecture in 1981 was "We Have Not Thought Hard Enough," and one of his articles was titled "Economic Ignorance Is No Excuse." He was even more blunt at times: "Sloppiness is not next to Godliness," he wrote in a 1984 essay. Christians need to know the structures of the world and thus must listen carefully to the people within these structures. We must be "first of all the listeners. And it is only by listening not only to the needs but also to the strengths of the laity that we'll get anywhere," he wrote. In the same piece is a subheading "The Laity are not Sheep." Gibbs put the matter positively in another article titled "That the Good May Be Clever": "[W]e must learn not only to be well-meaning, but also competent citizens."

Equipping the saints is a dominant motif in all of Gibb's work – his writing, his lecturing, and his involvement within institutions. He found that laypeople are open to learning: "The impressive thing about the most effective laity that I meet is their capacity to learn, their habit of learning all kinds of things in all kinds of ways." Such education has two dimensions: "...a constant attempt to assess the new knowledge, the new experience, the new challenge, against what has been called 'the mind of Christ,' the vision which we have – imperfect yet genuine – of what God wants done for us and for his world ..."

In addition to what the local parish offers, Gibbs insisted that other educational experiences are crucial for equipping Christians to serve Christ in the world. He particularly emphasized retreats, dialogues and arguments "about the issues in one's work" and "opportunities for some kind of Christian brainstorming about the future." Equipping means not only education but also the importance of being sustained in the faith as Christians encounter the messy complexity of their immediate world. Thus Gibbs recognized that gathering laity together for learning from one another and supporting one another was essential for the Christian community.

Gibbs himself was, if nothing else, a bridge who connected people and institutions. He accomplished this primarily through his volumi-

nous correspondence. The purpose of the letters was sometimes to enlist writers for one of his publications or to request persons or judicatories to support his work with laity. But more frequently his hand-written letters informed people that he was planning a gathering at a central location, such as Auburn Theological Seminary in New York City, and invited them to join the conversation. And leaders such as Jack White from the Lutheran Theological Seminary in Philadelphia, Dick

Gibbs in 1981.   Broholm from Andover Newton Theological Seminary, Bob Reber from Auburn, and a dozen others, including Lutheran lay leaders William Diehl and Nelvin Vos, would gather for information from Gibbs and mutual support. Richard Mouw described such a gathering and Gibbs' participation:

> A group of us, maybe ten or twelve, would show up in some retreat center and report on what was happening in the cause of the laity. We would often read something in preparation for theological discussion. Mark always acted kind of crotchety at these events, but we all had become very affectionate toward him. Once we were at a Catholic center where another group was having a silent weekend where their only mode of communication was to use Tinker Toys to express themselves. He was horrified. Another time, one of the denominational leaders in our group suggested an exercise where we would begin our time together answering two ques-

tions: Where would I rather be than at this meeting? And what is my worst worry about our project? People got into it, but when it was Mark's turn he answered the questions this way: "Where would I rather be? It is none of your damn business! What is my worst worry? That we will have to do more of this nonsense!"

Gibbs did not use the word "networking," but that was exactly the result of such meetings. To use another image, Gibbs was a kind of modern Paul who planted the laity movement as he traveled from place to place.

To work in partnerships with others is a deep need, as he and Morton wrote in *God's Frozen People*: "Nothing is more certain than that God intends his people to work in groups, in fellowships, together." Thus dialogue is essential, which these authors defined as "hammering out together the problems of life today."

Examples of Gibbs' commitment to dialogue were his involvement in two projects in the early 1980s, both underwritten by LAOS IN MINISTRY, a movement within the Lutheran Church in America from 1976 to 1988, when the Evangelical Lutheran Church in America was formed in another merger of U.S. Lutheran church bodies.

The first of these projects was a theological colloquium held in New York City in 1982 that called together about two dozen Lutheran theologians. The purpose was to strengthen the theological foundation of ministry of the laity. Each participant prepared a two- to three-page paper on such topics as "The Priesthood of all Believers" and "Calling in the New Testament." Gibbs launched the discussion with a keynote presentation, "No More Spiritual Babies: The Development of a Strong Laity," engaged in vigorous dialogue during the three-day meeting, and was the final respondent, carefully critiquing the entire undertaking with his characteristic directness. (The full text of Gibbs' keynote address is included in the Appendix.)

The second project entailed Gibbs visiting a good number of theological schools, including several of the seminaries of the Lutheran Church in America. Gibbs spent at least two days on each campus. He spoke in chapel and sat in on classes to talk with professors and students. His purpose was to take a kind of audit of the institution's commitment to nurturing the ministry of the laity. The result was an Audenshaw Paper, "The Signs That They Take the Laity Seriously: Theological Colleges and the Laity," a detailed and provocative piece which both constructively and critically assessed as a whole the strengths and weaknesses of the institutions he visited.

Gibbs carefully scrutinized the formal curriculum of the schools by exploring each of their offerings, for example, church history: "Such an institution tries to develop an understanding of the history of the whole People of God ... The laity are the forgotten and yet the enormous majority in church history." And he spent considerable time describing what should be elements of the "hidden curriculum" of a seminary:

> The college library reflects concerns for the whole *laos*.
> In its selection of books and periodicals, it is anxious to cover the ministries of laypeople as well as those of clergy, and it is concerned with Christian ministries and witness outside as well as inside the traditional parish structures ... Lay students are as a matter of course fully involved with seminary worship and community life. ...
> The college is anxious to use laity as teachers and resource people in full partnership with ordained people! And if it does so, it does not treat them as "second-class citizens" in policymaking committees and the like.

Gibbs ended his lengthy analysis by noting: "Occasionally, I must admit these visits to seminaries and theological colleges have been deeply disappointing; and in particular, the 'hidden curriculum' has seemed to weigh very heavily against any true partnership between the ordained and the unordained." However, he added: "I want to testify again, and again, ... I found a true desire – sometimes indeed a strong hunger – to find new ways of theological training which will produce 'strong pastors for strong laity,' clergy who know how to encourage and work with and *listen to* laypeople."

Gibbs not only engaged in conversation with groups but spent considerable time with individuals. William Diehl gives one illustration of Gibbs' eagerness to listen and learn from others:

> In my responsibilities as a national sales manager for Bethlehem Steel, I made trips to San Francisco. I always stayed at the Fairmont Hotel in the Towers. Whenever possible, Mark would come over from Vesper Society offices to have dinner with me. I can still picture our after-dinner chats in my twentieth-story suite overlooking California Street which ran down to the Embarcadero. We propped our chairs facing the breathtaking glitter of the city and sipped Mark's favorite Scotch as we talked about big business in America. Mark kept on asking me questions since he was aware that many people, including Christians, have stereotyped ideas about business and its practices. And he wanted to get it right.

The personal relationship with Gibbs was significant for Richard Mouw as well. His account provides deep insights into the profound influence Gibbs had on many individuals:

> Most important was that Mark became a dear friend. A rather strange friend, to be sure. He was never very warm – until near the end, which I will describe soon. He was always school-marmish with me: "You *will* do this ... you *will* read this." The relationship shaped me in significant ways. Reading Kraemer [*The Theology of the Laity*] was a major theological event for me. And I became a part of a movement – comprised in a special

way by the friends-of-Gibbs, that gave direction to a lot of what I have done theologically.

Mark was, in my mind, a saint – an itinerant Franciscan-type lay friar, whose mission in life was driven by a passionate commitment to upgrading the status of the laity in the theological understanding of the church. He was an ecumenist of a special sort, and he saw me as a key link to evangelicalism. While he often derided my Dutch Calvinism, he was genuinely interested in bringing my kind of Kuyperianism into the mix. His overall strategy seemed to be to bring various strands – post-Vatican II "Apostolate of the Laity" Yves Congar theology, the best of Lutheran vocation theology, the theological instincts that gave shape to so many vocation-specific laity groups in evangelicalism (Christian Nurses Fellowship, Christian Legal Society, Fellowship of Christian Athletes, etc.), Anglican insights about the meaning of baptism – into a rich interaction that could provide a broad-based movement to promote the cause of the laity as God's people in the world. ...

When I moved to Fuller [Theological Seminary] in 1985, Mark was upset with me. He felt strongly that my teaching at Calvin College was in essence an important exercise in the education of the laity for ministry. For me to move to a seminary was, for him, my running the risk of joining the enemy. We had good arguments about this.

A few months before he died, he came to visit me in Pasadena. I had not seen him for a while, and I was shocked at how frail he was. We spent several hours together in my office, and then at lunch. While he was very weak, he was still his school-marmish self. Until he was ready to leave. Then he thanked me for my friendship, and told me this was probably the last time we would see each other. "There is no need to be emotional about it," he said. But then he began to cry. "I have told you it was a mistake to come here to Fuller," he said. "But it does not have to be. You can promote the cause here, and it can have a big impact. Promise me you will stay faithful." I did, and I moved to give him a hug, but he turned and left.

A Life of Faith in Action

Gibbs became ill in 1984 and had two intestinal cancer operations. He was aware that the prognosis was terminal. But he continued on indefatigably.

In November 1985 Gibbs was honored at a huge convocation of 350 people on the ministry of the laity held at Andover Newton Theological Seminary near Boston. The citation reads: "Mark Gibbs, for his creation and nurturing of a worldwide network of persons, projects and institutions committed to the ministry the laity and his skill in writing and editing articles and books that have shaped the global movement." At the close of the gathering, the participants from fifteen Protestant denominations and the Roman Catholic Church signed a manifesto, "God's People in Ministry: A Call," which opened with this paragraph: "As people called by God, we respond by calling on ourselves and our churches to be the creative and living Body of Christ in the world. We affirm that the ministry of God's people in the world is the Church at work. We are the Church in the world." These words capture the essence of Gibbs' vocation.

And in these last months, he continued his correspondence with the large network of his colleagues by means of what he called over the years "Muker Memos," named for the small village that Gibbs called home. In December 1985 he wrote in Muker Memo No. 116: "This will be a shorter Muker Memo than usual, and most of our readers of course know why. The good news about my health in the last Memo has proved false, and the distinguished specialist in London was simply wrong in his diagnosis. In late August I had another and rather severe operation for colon cancer, and this time it is taking rather longer to recover from it, though I have started a prudent amount of travel again." The letter continues with three paragraphs filled with his travels and writing, including his ongoing editing of Laity Exchange Books.

To appreciate his continual energy, one only needs to look at his schedule for the months just before he died. Note that he attended a conference at the Evangelical Academy in Bad Boll just before his death on June 30.

Address List for Mark Gibbs, 1 April 1986 to:

1-7 April	Mostly Muker
8-10	Probably London
11-13	Muker
14-18	London and Chichester Theological College
19-22	Muker
23	Hinksey Centre, Oxford
24	Geneva
25	Basel
26 to 1 May	Mostly Muker
2	London
3-4	Kirchentag meeting, Fulda
5	London
6-7	New York
8-14	San Leandro
15-18	Christian Festival, Calgary
19-21	BCC Conference, High Leigh

22 to 2 June	Mostly Muker
3-5	Probably London
6-14	Mostly Muker
15-18	London
19-22	German-American Conference at Bad Boll Academy
23 to 3 July	Mostly Muker

These many-sided activities in five countries within a few months reveal a human being who dedicated his life to the very end to nurture the calling of the people of God to serve in God's world.

The Church Times ended its obituary, "Mark Gibbs: Champion of the Ministry of the Laity," by commenting on his deep commitment:

> Only a man of exceptional discipline and devotion could have accomplished so much with such limited administrative and financial support. His Christian commitment ran very deep; and the final phase of his life, when he travelled in much discomfort and pain as cancer exacted its toll, was heroic.
>
> He was, however, unable to suffer fools gladly, and his influence in Britain might have been greater had he been endowed with greater patience. But he believed passionately in the need for the Church to be de-clericalised, so that it might become a more effective instrument of the Christian mission, and he was not prepared to compromise on this fundamental point.

Bruce Johnson and his wife visited Gibbs in Muker just a few days before his death. "Even in his very weakened condition, Mark was still the nearly ideal British host in his rural cottage from which flowed so much valuable influence," Johnson said.

Ever the thoughtful gentleman, Gibbs phoned Robert Brorby just a few days before he died to inquire about Brorby's own health. "I appreciated the call," Brorby said. "I don't know if we said 'goodbye'; Mark was not the sentimental type."

Reuben Jessop, who was president of Vesper Society at the time, spent the last week of June in Muker. But Gibbs had caught a virus that he could not resist. He was taken to the hospital on a Sunday evening and died the following morning.

The day was June 30, 1986. A memorial service was held at the Episcopal Center in New York City on September 15, 1986, in which U.S. leaders participated. A memorial service was also held at the Manchester Cathedral on October 14, 1986, with Bishop Patrick Rodger conducting the service. Bishop Rodger had earlier served as executive secretary of the World Council of Churches from 1961-1966 as well as Bishop of Manchester from 1970-1978 and then became Bishop of Oxford from 1978-1986.

Gibbs and Bishop Rodger were close friends with common passions. Bishop Rodger had chaired an ecumenical group including Gibbs, which, according to Gibbs, consisted of a wide spectrum: "Evangelicals and Catholics and 'liberals,' clergy and laity, women and men." Sponsored by the Church of England Board of Education, the group issued a report in 1985 titled "Yes – All of Us Are Called," which later became the book *All Are Called*. Gibbs summarized the report in four single-spaced pages in Audenshaw Papers a year before his death. It is clear that he was not only enthusiastic about the contents of the report but also about the process: "It was quite extraordinary and very promising that we came very quickly to a basic agreement about the common calling of all Christians." The message of the report conveys the mission to which Gibbs devoted many years of his life:

> Nothing in our lives, not one of our activities or our
> times of rest and inactivity, is exempt from the claims of
> the Gospel and the intelligent application of Christian
> thinking and learning to it. Our attitude to politics,

trade, sex, television, sports or anything else must be grounded in a positive and joyful theology of God's creation. This is the heart of the gospel. This is the most refreshing news that human beings can hear: the proclamation of our common Christian dignity and our common Christian servanthood.

Two weeks after his death, *The Tablet*, a British Roman Catholic publication, carried a tribute that captures much of Gibbs' life and work:

> Gibbs gave himself to the very end to the cause of lay ministry. He had a hand in lay centres all over the world, writing, lecturing, stimulating, inspiring and irritating. The book he wrote with Ralph Morton is called *God's Frozen People* and his task was to unfreeze them. To this end, he spent half of his life in aeroplanes. The final sentence of a letter from him would most often be to the effect that he regretted not signing it personally but since dictating it, he had had to depart for such and such an airport. He had many friends who bore with his abrasiveness – he did not suffer fools gladly – appreciating that he was driven by a force which swept everything before it. He never married. There was a moment when he might have done so but he broke his engagement, just as he also gave up being a schoolmaster in spite of his extraordinary effect on his pupils. In truth he was married to his vocation. Perhaps the vocation was to some extent self-imposed but no one who knew him had any doubt of its validity. It was a Protestant vocation, restless, ruthless, deeply impressive ... He would never have realised that he had achieved a certain greatness, and perhaps in a sense it was indeed in spite of himself that he did so.

A letter from Dr. James G. Bryant dated May 28, 1986, written on behalf of the Board of Directors of Vesper Society just a month before

Gibbs' death, was intended, one assumes, not only to bid Gibbs farewell but also to encourage him by underscoring the board's commitment to the ministry of the laity:

> It is my privilege to write you on behalf of the Board of Directors of Vesper Society to thank you for your assistance and leadership as we have tried as laymen to spread the gospel, to perform good works, and to keep the faith. As a Board, despite our shortcomings, we have had our successes, as you know, for you have been a part of these successes.
>
> You have shared your faith with us and we have endeavored to share this faith with others in a like manner. Our faith is sometimes plagued by doubt, but it always contains more encouragement and hope. It is the encouragement and hope we now emphasize. ...
>
> Our Board membership has changed over the years but the concept of the ministry of the laity continues in the Vesper Society. We love the Lord. We love His work and we will continue to do our share. This work has drawn our lives and spirit more closely to God. We trust in God. We know He cares for us.
>
> May God bless you, keep you, and guide your labors done in His name.

Two weeks before his death, Gibbs responded:

> It was a great pleasure to have your kind and supportive letter of May 28th.
>
> It is becoming more difficult for me to work now, but I still expect to carry on for some more months; and indeed I have just managed to send the next *Laity Exchange* to press. ...
>
> It is very good of you to write on behalf of the Board, and I very much appreciate this. I am sure that you have the interests of the laity at heart as you plan for the future.

4

A SHIFTING LANDSCAPE

In September 1991, five years after Mark Gibbs' death, the future of the laity movement was uncertain. Sensing the need for conversation, Vesper Society convened a group of American laity leaders at Daylesford Abbey, a monastic community in Paoli, Pennsylvania, just outside Philadelphia where the Society was conceived. The participants arrived with that Gibbsian combination of ambition and frustration.

Thirty-two leaders, from more than eight different denominational backgrounds, answered the invitation to "develop national strategies for implementing the universally accepted principle that all baptized persons have been called into ministry." Among the participants were sociologist Robert Wuthnow, author William Diehl, Marketplace Ministry director Pete Hammond, and New Testament scholars Robert Banks and Joel Green.

Like Gibbs and his colleagues in Vesper Society, the Daylesford participants were frustrated that the institutional church had not fully embraced the ministry of the laity even after several decades of advocacy. The invitation to Daylesford posed a question that conveyed their frustration:

> Although many denominations, through official declarations, and most churches, through theological conviction, affirm that all Christians are called into ministry in all facets of daily life, why does it seem to

many that ministry appears to be primarily located in local church activity, and not identified frequently enough in the bustle of daily life?

Gibbs' critique of the church echoed in Daylesford Abbey, as did the sound of sadness and weariness. Diehl named the loneliness of movement leaders as "they struggled within institutional structures that paid little more than lip service to the imperative."

However, they were not content to simply complain. They wanted to do something. They wondered if progress might be achieved through greater collaboration among laity groups. The invitation posed a second question: "Can a healthy synergism develop through the cooperative efforts of the variety of organizations that exist to support the ministry of the laity in work, family and civic life?"

These two questions framed their three days of conversation. Yet even as they met, the landscape of American religious life was shifting. Profound changes were underway that would eclipse the laity's struggle with the institutional church and, consequently, sap some of the laity movement's organizing energy that had centered in institutional reform. Among those shifts was this reality: Christians increasingly claimed their vocation in the world – just as Gibbs and Vesper Society had envisioned – without waiting for the institutional church's support.

The institutional church was preoccupied with other concerns. By 1991 U.S. denominations were reeling from more than two decades of decline in membership and giving. The weakened structures were battered further by the hot-button social issues of the day – abortion and homosexuality. Local churches, intent on their own survival, began to innovate in worship and outreach ministries, often emphasizing the importance of lay leadership. While "ministry" was still understood primarily as an activity inside the local church and not "in the bustle of daily life," as the Daylesford participants observed, a fundamental shift in options for laypeople occurred. If in previous decades laypeople essentially stood outside the doors of the institutional church, knocking and asking for affirmation and opportunity, now other doors swung open.

Increasingly, laypeople found multiple ways to express their vocation in the world, and these options widened following Daylesford. Indeed, in the years since 1991, American Christianity has experienced far-reaching changes that underscore the significance of laypeople, or rather all Christians, having a ministry in the world. For instance, the growth of megachurches, which in many settings emphasize that every member is a minister, has inspired Christian reflection and action on vocation. *The Purpose-Driven Life*, by megachurch founder Rick Warren, pastor of Saddleback Church in Lake Forest, California, is one of the best-selling books of all time. Founded in 1980, Saddleback is now a global player in fighting AIDS and addressing poverty, disarming earlier critiques of megachurches as lacking a larger social vision. In the summer of 2008, Saddleback sponsored, and Warren moderated, the first joint appearance of presidential candidates Barack Obama and John McCain.

Other changes since Daylesford have been equally influential: the advent of the "emerging church," where small communities of Christians blend worship and service and creatively engage secular culture; and the widening of the "invisible church," that church-in-the-world where countless people live out their faith, even in secular structures that are surprisingly receptive to spirituality. These changes have generally produced the very results Gibbs and Vesper Society sought: churches focused more on the gifts of the people; interest in the intersection of faith and work deepened; and many Christians took up the question of their vocation in the world with renewed vigor. In effect, much of what Gibbs and Vesper Society had called for came to pass, even as some of the catalyzing energy of the laity movement – that energy invested in the battle for institutional recognition – dissipated.

Daylesford, therefore, offers a unique vantage point to look backward and forward. From here we can further discern what motivated Gibbs and Vesper Society and observe how their common passion led to particular activities. These activities reflected changing times. Indeed, seismic social, cultural and political changes were already in motion when Gibbs and the Society forged their relationship in 1970. So we have to retrace some of the ground covered in earlier chapters to bring into greater relief this shifting landscape. From Daylesford we turn toward our own time and glimpse other changes, for Vesper Society and for the larger laity movement. By tracing the development of the Society, itself a bellwether of the laity movement, we might ascertain what happened to the larger thrust, that ambitious and collective calling of every Christian to be, as Gibbs said, partners with God in "the fashioning of a new humanity."

Catalytic Conversations

At Daylesford Abbey, Vesper Society did what it has always done best: it convened people for meaningful conversation. Sensing the need for dialogue about the state of the laity movement, the Society issued an invitation to the movement's leading figures, with no predetermined outcomes. Aside from some minimal structure of advance reading and presentations by Wuthnow, there was simply discussion – around a diagnosis of issues and a prescription for moving forward. The participants trusted the process.

Since its founding in 1965, the Society has understood its primary role as a convener, bringing leaders together for dialogue about critical issues, from healthcare ethics to peace in Latin America to the role of the Internet in faith-based organizations. The conversations are catalytic. Solutions emerge. Projects are born. Through it all, leaders make sense of their vocation in the world. Convening, then, is no small matter.

In Mark Gibbs the Society found a partner who shared this appreciation for the power of conversation. Gibbs' life was truly built around conversation. He devoted his time to planning conversations, to writing that provided a springboard for conversation, and to voluminous correspondence in between meetings. As he traveled from England to Germany and to the U.S., he left vigorous discussions in his wake.

In his books and essays for *Vesper Exchange* and *Laity Exchange*, Gibbs carried on the conversation. It was a discussion that Christians hungered for in the 1960s through the 1980s. He gave voice to what many people yearned to express: the frustration with the institutional church, with its "failure to understand that the church in mission and ministry is primarily the Christian layperson in the secular world at work and at leisure," as Robert Brorby put it. Gibbs also articulated the aspiration of many Christians, including the Society's founders: to build "truly human structures and societies for tomorrow and the day after tomorrow," as he wrote in *Christians With Secular Power*.

That vision required conversation. Although group discussion is sometimes disparaged as "mere talk," for Gibbs and the Society conversation was radical. Dialogue provided the occasion for lay leaders to claim their power; it gave them the space to affirm their ministry in the world and inspired them to act. They would not wait for the institutional church to create the forum. They convened the conversation themselves, thereby asserting their priesthood as believers and declaring the vision they would pursue as frontline followers of Christ – a vision of structures and societies that were truly serving people in the world in genuinely human yet effective ways, reflecting the loving care of God.

The conversation refined the vision and inspired action. As leaders grappled with difficult political and ethical issues in Society-sponsored dialogues, they made the vision concrete. Gibbs and the Society rejected a kind of sentimental view of the laity's ministry, namely, as Gibbs wrote in *Christians With Secular Power*, that their vocation is limited to "the personal, loving, affectionate responsibilities to family, friends, and neighbors." Gibbs and the Society wanted more. They wanted to exercise their power in the world. Like other leaders in the U.S. and Europe, they wanted to let go of a Christianity which "pretends that weakness is strength"; instead, they sought to use their power in business, education, politics and media, to put faith in action "by a matching of deep convictions and hard thinking," as Gibbs wrote elsewhere. "[T]he world has to be run, somehow," he noted. So Christians should be in on it.

The Society answered Gibbs' challenge. Using the San Leandro hospital as a base, and later a second hospital in nearby Hayward, the Society set about creating an arena for leaders to practice their faith. Here the Society engaged laypeople in reflecting and acting on the link between faith and health. The organization encouraged a broad definition of health – "not only a matter of caring for specific illnesses, but ... also a concern for the relief of social and environmental sickness," according to a 1976 Society report – and it called employees to a level of proficiency marked by outstanding healthcare delivery plus a "real sensitivity to the needs of the people and area" served by the hospital. The Society championed "corporate social responsibility" long before the concept entered public discourse.

For the Society's leaders, the hospital was a laboratory of their own making where they could cultivate the kind of Christian reflection that Gibbs advocated and which they knew was vital for laypeople and clergy alike. So the Society brought seminary students into the hospital for a yearlong program of service and education, making the hospital a locus of theological reflection and action for both ministerial students and lay professionals. Vesper Interns, who represented Protestant, Catholic and Jewish traditions, participated in seminars, shadowed doctors, and engaged in social service work in the community. The experience helped ministerial students "discover the significance of different professional roles and responsibilities in secular and non-church structures," said Eugene Heckathorn in a 1971 article. Through Vesper Residency, clergy who wanted a second occupational skill found employment at the San Leandro hospital for up to two years – an opportunity for "continuing education," as Heckathorn called it.

Tapping Gibbs' connections, the Society built a small dental clinic on the campus of Knox College in Spaldings, Jamaica. The Society recruited dentists for one-year appointments through a partnership with the University of California at San Francisco. By 1976 the Society had placed volunteer doctors, dentists and nurses in other countries: Liberia, Malawi, Lesotho, Antigua, Grenada and Bolivia.

Using its influence as a healthcare provider, the Society engaged other Bay Area health leaders in reflection upon innovation and ethics. Vesper Seminars explored such issues as population control, Third World health, and organizational development. The conversations were not esoteric. Like Gibbs, the Society's leaders were not interested in what their British friend called a "liberal debating forum." They used the seminars to elicit new knowledge and apply that knowledge to meeting human needs.

As the Society connected with Gibbs and found new conversation partners in the German Academies, the topics widened: Cold War politics, nuclear disarmament, U.S.-European relationships, international business ethics. Inspired by a 1979 pre-Kirchentag conference at Bad Boll on "Christian Concern for Health Care" and the European "Quest for Health" project, Society leaders returned to California to initiate their own "Quest for Health," a three-year program of seminars that explored the scientific, spiritual, political and economic dimensions of health in the U.S.

Dr. Alvin S. Rudisill, a member of the San Leandro hospital board, chaplain at the University of Southern California, and associate professor in USC's medical and religion schools, chaired the Quest for Health. Writing in 1982 at the conclusion of the project, which included healthcare professionals as well as consumers and providers in fourteen sessions, Rudisill said Vesper Society believed that "great ethical issues can best be addressed when concerned responsible persons of varying views come together in dialogue." And he underscored the effect of these conversations:

> While the Society has never structured these activities and events so that action was mandated, it is true that the Society consciously sees itself as a catalyst for action in at least two ways: (1) encouraging informed and renewed persons to leave the dialogues and *act* in their own ways in their spheres of influence; and (2) developing viable models of innovative programs in healthcare delivery which others might evaluate and emulate.

Such conversations gave the Society an outlet for its ambition: to be on the cutting edge, in the world, leading as Christians. Gibbs and Heckathorn articulated the organizational dimensions of this ambition in their essay "The Development of Large-Scale Corporate Caring," written as a position paper for consideration at the 1973 Kirchentag in Düsseldorf. The opening sentences, from two leaders not content to play church, were characteristically provocative:

> It is clear that our society requires the development of large-scale nonprofit and charitable organizations, which can match the complexity of governmental, business and economic and social life today. Such organizations have to develop what has been called a style of statistical compassion; preserving a genuine humanity in their operations and yet at the same time developing managerial competence and financial efficiency.

Gibbs and Heckathorn called charitable organizations to task for lagging behind business and government in their management practices. "It is distressing to find many religious and 'do-good' institutions caring for people in sloppy, unthoughtful and even callously mechanical ways." They encouraged the church and its charitable organizations to learn from the world, to make use of secular knowledge about leadership and communication, to seek the advice of laypeople who are deeply involved in such secular work, rather than only asking them "to help in relatively trivial ways." This was a matter of being smart and getting the theology right, Gibbs and Heckathorn argued.

> Christian theology maintains that God often speaks through secular people and institutions quite outside church structures and organizations. Therefore it is very necessary to learn everything we can from the most helpful secular wisdom we can find – and we must make deliberate efforts to look for it.

They summed up their essay with the words of John W. Gardner – "Accomplishing social change is work for the tough-minded and the competent," echoing Gibbs' observation quoted earlier: "[W]e must learn not only to be well-meaning, but also competent citizens."

The Society could back up this talk. It turned around the financially troubled San Leandro hospital, increasing the number of patients served annually from 5,000 in 1965 to almost 37,000 in 1973. The Society added innovative services in cardiopulmonary rehabilitation and family-centered maternity care. It built an eye surgery center and started a home health care program. In 1978, the same year that the Society acquired a second hospital in nearby Hayward, the organization launched one of the first hospice care programs in the U.S.

Ownership of the hospitals, though not planned at the start of the Society in 1965, "played right in and fit like a glove" in terms of giving laypeople opportunities to apply their faith, said co-founder Bob Cummings. Outside of the institutional church, the hospitals gave the Society's leaders a platform to act upon their aspirations. They were driven to make this happen for themselves. Again, they could not wait for the church to get it.

In 1980, in the 10th anniversary edition of *Vesper Exchange*, Robert
Brorby articulated the Society's ambition, as noted earlier:

> Ten years ago, one of us would occasionally say, "Today
> San Leandro, tomorrow the world." Although we said
> that in jest, it expresses a truth about the Society. We are
> not egomaniacs. We realize that our major work will be
> through institutions in that part of the world in which
> they are located. Today that is East Oakland, San
> Leandro, and Hayward, California. This is a small slice
> of the world. But our interests transcend those commu-
> nities. We want to help train seminarians. We want to
> be a force in the movement of the laity, as the laity relate
> their religious faith to their daily life. We want to see
> this happen not only in our institutions, but throughout
> the world.

Their ambition flowed from a sense of duty. Gibbs called that "lay
responsibility," the idea that "religious obligations will inevitably lead us
into acute controversies and responsible compromises," to journey into
the structures of the world, often through "difficult and foggy and
swampy territory." Brorby called this "service," and he said it motivated
the development of the Society's programs. As the organization entered
the 1980s, Brorby expected service to be central. "We hope that at the
decade's end we will have been good stewards," he said.

Pursuing Multiple Passions

In 1983 *The Daily Review* of Hayward began a story on Vesper
Society with the following observation: "It might seem odd for a health
care organization to jump feet first into issues of disarmament,
apartheid and business ethics. But Vesper Society does just that." Why?
Bruce Johnson, then vice president of the Society, responded: "We
(Vesper Society) are primarily a health-care corporation, but in a broad-

er sense the health of the world depends on this continuing process (of dialogue)." Johnson noted, "It's easy to withdraw, to say, 'Let me run my little hospice in San Leandro.'" But the Society could not take that route. Gibbs described such leaders in *Christians With Secular Power*: "They ache to relate their Christian faith to the power struggles and opportunities and corruptions of the structures of government and industry. They have some Christian hope left, and more than a faint vision of truly human structures and societies for tomorrow and the day after tomorrow."

By the mid-1980s the Society's activities reflected the diversity of passions among lay Christians. The organization's letterhead alone signaled its multiple interests. Under the Vesper Society logo was a long list of programs: Home Care, Hospice, Child Care Consulting Services, Management Consultants for Industry and Business, Health Education, Laity Information Service, Laity Seminars and Programs, Athletic Club and Wellness Center, and Auxiliary. "We were broadly based and involved in many things," said Cummings, who recalled that as new activities were proposed, the question Vesper Society would ask was, "Do we have a ministry there?"

That palpable passion was symbolized in the Society's logo – a flame representing Moses' encounter with the burning bush in the third chapter of Genesis. When God called to Moses out of the bush to rescue God's people, Moses had all sorts of reasons why he could not possibly do this thing. For the members of Vesper Society, the story represented the dilemma of the layperson, facing the mystery of the call of God to serve in the world, totally unsure of what to do and how to do it, being told ultimately to rely on the help of God. That burning bush became the symbol of the Society's work.

The Society's actions paralleled the moves made by other Christians around the world from the 1950s through the 1980s. The Academies in Germany, the Christian Frontier Council that Gibbs joined in 1953, other frontier groups in Australia, India, Japan, and elsewhere, Christian business networks, and associations of church-related non-profit organizations – all were, in one measure, attempts to bypass the institutional church's intransigence and declare the ministry of the laity in the world. Such special-purpose groups grew considerably in the U.S. from the 1960s on. Organized around particular interests or professions, these groups provided a place for lay leaders to affirm and encourage each other. In this regard, Vesper Society itself was a special-purpose group. Gibbs cautioned denominational leaders not to interfere here, but rather recognize that laypeople could have "multiple loyalties" that included the local church as well as these outside groups. By 1988 Robert Wuthnow, writing in *The Restructuring of American Religion*, observed that for some Christians, participation in these special-purpose groups could be a viable expression of church alongside membership in a denomination or attendance in local worship.

During this same period, nonprofit organizations like Vesper Society grew exponentially in the U.S. Many nonprofit groups tapped federal funds to start or expand operations in health care, housing, and other social services. Society co-founder Cummings was in the thick of this expansion as a developer of affordable housing for seniors. Cummings chaired the Subsection on Housing for the 1971 White House Conference on Aging. One result of the growth of the nonprofit sector was that opportunities for mission-driven work increased significantly. Although clergy often started church-related nonprofits, by the 1970s and 1980s lay professionals took the reins and began to reshape the conversation about ministry in ways that Gibbs and Heckathorn had envisioned: effective service in the world was about marrying missional aspirations with the best in management practices.

These trends – the rise of special-purpose groups and the growth of the nonprofit sector – were but two signs that the landscape for the laity movement had shifted dramatically. While many lay leaders continued to hold onto their denominations like Jacob grasping the angel until it would bless him, the very fact that lay leaders could do the work of the church outside the institutional church meant that the movement was free to chart its own course. When Gibbs and Vesper Society forged their relationship in 1970, the conversation was largely about getting the institutional church to pay attention to the laity. Cummings noted that laypeople had to fight "to have the church open its doors in ways that only laypeople can fill them." But by the late 1980s, lay leaders had other options besides struggling with the institutional church for recognition.

The business world, for instance, warmed to discussions of spirituality and ethics. The Sullivan Principles, developed by Baptist minister Leon Sullivan to ensure that companies operating in South Africa promoted human rights, led U.S. firms to divest from South Africa in the mid-1980s in protest of the government's apartheid system. The first national Symposium on Servant Leadership was held in 1988, eighteen years after former AT&T executive Robert Greeleaf developed the concept of the servant leader. Greenleaf proposed that the well-being of others is the central concern of a servant leader, a proposal welcomed by many business leaders in the 1980s. Interest in moral leadership and ethical behavior grew, in part, in the wake of political and corporate scandals. Yet this interest was due also to the sense that leadership could embody one's deepest values, even in the rough and tumble world of commerce.

As an academic discipline and a major topic of conversation within corporate America, business ethics took off. The Society for Business Ethics was formed in 1980. By the middle of the decade, 40,000 students were enrolled in approximately 500 business ethics courses around the country, according to University of Kansas professor Richard T. De George's essay "A History of Business Ethics." Many of the nation's largest companies adopted ethics codes. Theological institutions started paying attention to this shift. Rod Lorimer, who chaired Vesper Society's board from 2005 through 2008, was a senior executive with The Clorox Company in the late 1980s when Otto Bremer, a professor and associate of the Society, invited Lorimer to speak on business ethics in a class at Pacific Lutheran Theological Seminary in Berkeley.

One might naturally assume that Gibbs, staked out as he was on the border of church and culture, saw these changes coming. Norman Lear, television and film producer, underscored the irony that business was now the "fountainhead of values" in American society. "If the church was the focal point for personal values and public mores in medieval times, that role has been assumed, unwittingly perhaps, by the modern corporation," Lear said in an address to Harvard's Kennedy School of Government in 1987. That doubtless overstated the case by some distance, but it was true that conversation about ethics in business was now widespread and that many Christians were leading those conversations, not only in the U.S. but in Europe as well.

In 1989, for instance, Ridley Hall, the Anglican theological college at Cambridge University, established its Faith in Business project, which continues today. According to the project's Web site, the initiative "developed out of a twin concern that the concept of lay ministry is too often restricted to what laypeople can do for the church (rather than taking in the work which occupies most of their time), and that the church's attitude to business savours too much of indifference, suspicion or hostility." Gibbs had voiced the same concerns and called for Christian engagement in business. "It needs to be said plainly and emphatically that in principle there is nothing against, and much for, Christian laity playing a major part in the power networks and structures of business enterprises," he wrote.

Again, Vesper Society answered Gibbs' challenge. In 1988 and 1989, the Society and Oxford-based Hinksey Centre sponsored conferences on international business ethics in Anaheim, California, and

Cambridge. In 1990 the Society joined Hinksey in a conference on "Just Profits" and issued ethical guidelines for international corporations. That same year the Mark Gibbs Memorial Lecture featured sociologist Robert Bellah on the theme "Discipleship and Citizenship in the Workplace."

On this frontier of church and culture, one could see how significantly the landscape had shifted for the laity movement. While the institutional church hadn't caught on, there were new openings for lay engagement in secular structures. Having tired of their frustration with the institutional church's lack of understanding, Christian laypeople began to shift the center of their ministry activities to other arenas. In short, when Vesper Society and other leaders of the laity movement arrived at Daylesford in 1991, they were dealing with a different world.

A 'Post-Laity' Era?

Harlan Stelmach, then president and CEO of Vesper Society, captured a moment at Daylesford when the conversation stumbled over language. The scene was one more sign of change to come:

> At a particularly comic, yet poignant moment in the Daylesford Consultation, one of the nonprofessionally based "lay leaders" (i.e., someone not getting paid to be a lay leader, or someone with a job in "the real world" and not a professional advocate for lay ministry, or a second-class or "amateur" minister of the church) realized that in this gathering he was a lay lay leader, meaning that he was a nonprofessional-nonprofessional minister, or an amateur-amateur in his ministerial vocation.

Writing after Daylesford in *Laity Exchange*, Stelmach said it was no wonder the group eliminated the word "laity" from the declaration it issued; instead, the participants opted for "ministry in daily life." Stelmach noted while the word laity comes from *laos*, "all the people of

God," the word has long been used to distinguish clergy from non-ordained church members. Some lay leaders reinforced this split in their historical struggle for affirmation, while others betrayed a "deep (and at times justified) anti-clericalism" in their use of the word laity, Stelmach said. He wondered if the language confusion at Daylesford pointed to the "dead end of a laity movement separated too militantly in language and fact from the clergy." He added, "Perhaps we are on the verge of a post-laity movement."

The Daylesford participants may have recognized that something beyond language was at stake. They commented on how far the movement had come, in spite of meager support from the denominations. They underscored how many of the movement's aspirations had become reality. "The territory for ministry is as wide as the territory for human activity and effort," wrote Clyde Evans of the National Center for the Laity, an independent Roman Catholic organization, following Daylesford. The movement's infusion in society, which is just what Gibbs and Vesper Society sought, ironically pointed to a "post-laity" era, to borrow Stelmach's phrase. A new day was drawing near when the old institutionally determined language of "clergy" and "laity" would no longer be relevant, chiefly because the myriad expressions of Christian vocation would be less dependent on the institutional church and its categories. Christians could pursue all manner of ministry on their own – irrespective of the institution's understanding or its blessing. Writing after Daylesford, Marnette Saz of the Andover Newton Center for the Ministry of the Laity put it this way: "The ministry of all believers has become the daily life of so many that it cannot be stopped now."

Still, at Daylesford, while there was the residue of a desire to convince the denominations to truly demonstrate they believed in and supported the ministry of the whole people of God, there was an even stronger conviction that "more must be done," and if not by the institutional church, then other vehicles would have to be found. The

Daylesford participants issued the following declaration:

> We, the participants of the 1991 Consultation on Ministry in Daily Life, affirm that all Christians have been called into ministry and that, for most of them, the arena of ministry is in and to the world.
>
> We believe that more must be done to help Christians to discern and claim their ministries and to be affirmed, equipped, supported and empowered in them.
>
> To these ends, we commit ourselves to continue advocacy of the ministry of the whole church. We will work with each other, whenever practical, in developing and providing resources, offering events, doing research, sharing programs and learnings, and maintaining a network which will translate the rhetoric of Ministry in Daily Life into reality in the lives of our brothers and sisters in the faith.

Daylesford inspired the launch of the Coalition for Ministry in Daily Life, which initially focused on advocating for greater institutional support. This broadly international ecumenical network, which includes Roman Catholic organizations and Evangelicals as well as mainstream churches, continues to be one of the key organizations within the ministry in daily life movement. The Coalition's purpose is "fostering the affirmation and practice of ministry in daily life by all followers of Christ." It publishes a newsletter, *Laynet*, holds an annual consultation, and promotes Internet-based sharing groups. All in all, this network owes its origin partly to Vesper Society's sponsorship of the Daylesford Consultation.

For Vesper Society, Daylesford was a turning point. Seven years before, the Society had sold its two hospitals and created a private operating foundation. No longer bound by the responsibility of managing two institutions, the Society was free to give its full attention to the mission of promoting God's demand for social justice throughout the world. After Daylesford, in his reflections on a "post-laity movement," Stelmach noted that Vesper Society was engaged in a strategic planning process to sort out its future. The organization had identified four questions to shape its planning:

> What is our religious focus?
>
> How do we relate to a pluralistic environment?
>
> Is it empowering laity?
>
> Is it empowering all the ministries of the church?

"Civil society" became the larger theme for the organization's activities. The search for the common good, a conversation that includes many players, religious and secular, provided an umbrella under which the Society would have latitude to chart its particular course, wrote Stelmach, summarizing the contribution of Society board member Robert Marshall, former president of the Lutheran Church in America:

> Conceivably, moral discourse in civil society would encompass the broadest imaginable scope. In any one activity or for a particular span of time, Vesper might choose to concentrate on one aspect of the discourse, or a particular combination of factors, always remaining aware of the comprehensiveness of its mission and open to alternatives and the possibility of new emphases in its activities.
>
> For Vesper, moral discourse normally seeks to relate religious faith to daily life and to the involvements that people have with social structures and institutions. Vesper involves persons of various religious faiths, in order that moral discourse may include interfaith dialogue as a means to promote the common good.
>
> Optimally, development of the common good benefits

from moral discourse among all those who have a
share in society. With this conviction, Vesper seeks to
bring together persons who represent a wide variety of
viewpoints, experiences, and roles in society, and who
share a commitment to moral discourse for the common good.

Stelmach concluded, "The Daylesford Consultation has helped us
begin to understand new ways of perceiving the *laity* movement in the
United States."

Stelmach urged the Society's international friends to likewise
devote their efforts to the "ethics of the common good." Writing in
preparation for the first World Convention of Christian Lay Centres
and Movements, held in Montreat, North Carolina, in September of
1993, Stelmach said it is "incontrovertible" that all Christians are called
to live out their faith in the world. "The larger and more important
question," he said, "is, what should we be about together in the world?"
His answer: "to help promote the common good."

That language of "the common good" and "civil society" came into
wider usage in the early 1990s among political, academic, religious and
nonprofit leaders. For Christians committed to ecumenism and interfaith cooperation, the idea of a common good opened up the possibility
of ethical and moral reflection in increasingly secular and interfaith
contexts. Like Vesper Society, others in the laity movement, such as the
European laity centers and the Kirchentag, embraced this new vision.
In the common good they saw the promise of meaningful work and
community amid pluralism.

Thus, as Vesper Society moved into the 1990s, it focused more on
the cultivation of civil society. Within that framework, it continued to
work on health issues, specifically the provision of health care for the
underserved; but for the most part, the Society set aside its work of
intentionally convening laypeople for reflection on their ministry in

the world. The Society held the last Mark Gibbs Memorial Lecture in 1995.

Interestingly, a Gibbs lectureship, sponsored by the Association for Laity Centres, continued for another decade in Great Britain, until declining attendance prompted the association to end the series. With funds from the dissolution of the Audenshaw Foundation, the William Temple Foundation supported a Gibbs Fellow for a time, and the University of Manchester established a scholarship in Gibbs' memory to assist doctoral students working on practical theology, specifically the engagement of laypeople in the world beyond the church. That scholarship continues to this day. Yet in Great Britain and throughout Europe, there was a noticeable shift in the energy and interests of the laity movement. Leaders turned toward other opportunities, just as Vesper Society did.

However – and this is important to note – most of the Society's projects involved laypeople. The Society's board and staff as well as the organization's project partners were nearly all laity. And the Society's work continued to be about that larger vision promoted by Gibbs: to engage secular structures from a Christian perspective in order to make the world a better place. But how to do this was, and is, a source of board debate. "We disagree and sometimes therefore it has affected our decision-making process quite a bit," said board member Barbara Varenhorst in a recent interview. "But we disagree how we should save the world."

That passion for social justice was exemplified in the 1990s through the Society's peacemaking work in Central America. In 1994, for instance, the Society helped bring together factions in Guatemala's long-running civil war. Meeting at the Presidio in San Francisco, the discussions were moderated by former Costa Rican President and Nobel Laureate Oscar Arias, who noted, "After the end of the Cold War, to continue with one that has been going on in Guatemala for 30 years is an anachronism" (*San Francisco Examiner*, October 4, 1994). Gaspar Ilom, leader of an alliance of rebel groups, said that having a dialogue with military leaders was "a major stride forward that will be remembered in the history of Guatemala."

Varenhorst, who became interim president of the Society in 1996, recalled how the organization helped Guatemalan military, government, business, labor and academic leaders bring peace to their country. "We provided the finances to bring them together. We paid for the facilitator of their choice," she said. However, she noted, "We didn't tell them what they should do." Through a series of "roundtable" discussions, the participants demonstrated a respect and commitment to each other that was remarkable, she added. "Vesper made this possible by convening and setting the whole thing up and not facilitating it for them but providing the infrastructure so that could happen," she said.

The Guatemalan roundtables illustrated the Society's approach: to tackle an issue with some "practical means," Varenhorst explained, and "empowering the people who have to deal with that problem." Empowerment suggested a larger aim; in this idea the Society discovered a common theme running through its varied projects. "Inadvertently, not consciously, we were working on leadership issues," Varenhorst said. Leadership development became the "clothes string" from which the Society hung a variety of projects, she said.

Leadership development was explicit in 1999 when, under the direction of President Judith Larsen, the Society created a program for leaders in church-related health and human service organizations. The yearlong Ecumenical Leadership Institute, which continues today as the Faith-Based Leadership Institute, was designed to support the application of faith values to daily life. The program engaged mid-level and senior leaders in thinking theologically and practically about how they and their organizations could be faithful and effective – clear echoes of Gibbs and Heckathorn's 1973 essay. One recent participant said she was "losing steam" after fifteen years in the business of caring for troubled families and children. But the program helped her regain energy by teaching her to pause amid her busy schedule in order to reflect on the meaning of the work. Participants noted how the program supported them in connecting faith and service. "This learning experience gave me confidence in my leadership and enabled me to better articulate and live the values of the organization," said another leader.

Leadership development – the kind of critical education and significant ongoing support Gibbs had envisioned for laypeople – was also integral to the Society's Christian Community of Mesoamerica (CCM) project. The three-year initiative from 2001-2003 connected seventeen Central American faith-based organizations in a peer-directed learning model. CCM's focus was to improve "the quality of life for Central American communities marginalized by poverty and the consequences of civil war and natural disasters," according to the project's summary report. A critical first step was to strengthen the capacity of the members to respond to this mission – in other words, to develop leadership. Maria Elena Riddle, who managed the project for the Society, noted that some of the network members were nonprofits that formed out of congregations. They were lay groups and were responding from a place of faith and Christian values, she said. Trainings began with reading of scripture and prayer, with references to helping create God's kingdom on earth.

Similarly, the Masangane Treatment Program, a current Society-funded project in the Eastern Cape of South Africa, serves people with HIV and AIDS by combining anti-retroviral drug therapy with the rituals of a Christian community. Masangane's faith practices are important for healing and well-being, according to the Society and its partners, including the African Religious Health Assets Program. Under the leadership of President Mary Olson Baich, Vesper Society has played a significant role in drawing global attention to such assets

– the disease-fighting resources already present through the practices, networks and institutions of faith communities.

Other Society projects have been less explicit in linking faith with service. The Adolescent Health Initiative, launched in 2004, draws together three community organizations in Hayward, California, to improve the lives of underserved citizens through individual and family counseling. In 2005 the Society partnered with Sutter Delta Medical Center to open an urgent care clinic in Antioch, California, that serves the uninsured and working poor. These projects and others, though not explicitly laity programs, certainly embody ministry in daily life.

Nancy Nielsen, who led the Society's programs in the 1990s to connect health professionals and congregations, said that ministry of the laity was never a conscious focus; yet these programs and more recent ones have largely been about people of faith working together. For instance, Network 21, a technology-training program run by the Society from 1999-2003, convened leaders of Christian laity and retreat centers around the world. Known today as Oikosnet, this network of centers has also partnered with the Society on a mediation training program called Dialogue for Peaceful Change. In all of these projects, laypeople have been engaged and their commitment to vocation has deepened; however the projects are not explicitly expressed in terms of ministry in daily life as such but rather are focused on specific work toward the compassionate world that Christians yearn for: peacemaking, integrating faith and health, developing leaders, strengthening skills and networks, providing healthcare services.

Is this not the vision Mark Gibbs and Vesper Society articulated years ago? Gibbs and the Society wanted to serve the church, not by simply supporting the church's institutions but by answering their call within secular structures. Along with their friends in the laity movement, Gibbs and the Society believed it was possible for Christians to have faith in the world.

But sustaining this affirmation is no simple task. As noted at Daylesford, the challenge is to translate the rhetoric of ministry in daily life into reality in the lives of Christians. Individuals may not understand their role as "ministry" if their activities in daily life are not recognized as such by others. They may need help in seeing their daily life in that light as a response to God's call.

The task is further complicated by the comprehensiveness of ministry in daily life. "If we affirm that every Christian is a minister, do we mean that everything a Christian does is ministry?" they asked at Daylesford. Gibbs apparently had an answer: "[W]e must hold to the great truth that God calls us to a first-class style of life in *everything* we do, whether it is our worship or our work or our sports and entertainments and holidays, our eating and drinking and loving," he wrote in "Saturday's Ministries," a 1982 essay. "Nothing is exempt, until the hour of our death."

Gibbs made an audacious claim. And he captured the imagination of Vesper Society and the larger laity movement. Discerning how to be the people of God in all times and all places, including secular structures, was the shared work of Gibbs and the Society. Confident of their call, and empowered by a kind of holy ambition, Gibbs and the Society, along with countless other Christians, moved out into the world in service in the latter half of the 20th century. A prayer quoted by Gibbs in *Christians With Secular Power* may well have accompanied them:

> We are new men and women in Christ,
> Members of his Body, the world Church,
> Citizens of the Kingdom of God.
> We are called
> We are free
> We are rich
> We are sent

We are ministers, servants.

Lord help us to fulfill our ministries.

Amen

5

'MORE MUST BE DONE'

When Vesper Society and leaders of the laity movement gathered at Daylesford in 1991, significant changes were underway in the church and world. Those present began to realize that continued complaining about the church's lack of attention to the ministry of the laity was not enough – it was time to recognize that Christians were increasingly claiming their ministry rather than waiting for the church's blessing. This attitude, of course, as noted in Chapter 4, was very much in keeping with the spirit of Gibbs and the founders of Vesper Society – claiming rather than complaining, acting rather than waiting.

At the same time, something else was happening that has profound long-term implications for the ministry in daily life movement. The church itself was losing its central role in society, its traditional organizational structures losing their power and influence in the lives of people. A recent online survey of the 18- to 25-year-old millennial generation includes a question about the religious orientation of the responder, asking "Are you Religious, Spiritual, Agnostic, Atheist, Undecided, Uninterested?" In the early days of Vesper Society, such a survey would simply have asked what denomination the respondent belonged to; "Uninterested" would not likely have been a choice! In addition, the inclusion of "Spiritual" as a choice reflects a rather pervasive climate in today's world of a generalized sense of the divine.

We suggest that these changes represent both a crisis and an opportunity for Christians in the 21st century.

Consider first why this new situation is a crisis. The founders of Vesper Society and their colleague Mark Gibbs were not simply trying to be "good" laypeople in the world – they wished to be *Christian* laypeople in the world. Their motivation, their intentionality – their particularity – flowed from a sense of Christian vocation, calling. This is not to say that they were driven by a zeal for evangelism and conversions; but they certainly understood the need for Christians to be *God's* hands and feet and voices in the messiness of the world. They were being the church in the world, while being anchored in their congregations and church structures, nourished by Word and Sacraments through the organized church.

At Daylesford, Robert Wuthnow held up as one model of the future church the "invisible church," where people express their Christianity "not by doing church work, but by doing work, by being a physician, or a social worker, or being an engineer." But the founders of Vesper Society were interested in more than being good workers (in their case, businessmen). They were really being the church, on Monday as well as Sunday. They were acting out of a motivation to express their faith by being competent and effective businessmen engaged in carrying out God's work in the world by serving the poor, the lonely, the broken with the good news that the creator of the universe cares about them. Such a motivation is more than a general desire to do good by improving the condition of other human beings, as laudatory as that general desire is. It is more than a desire to be an ethical banker, a competent teacher, a careful builder of houses. There is a particularity about the way they lived, and that particularity was rooted in Word and Sacraments. If the institutional church is no longer as important in the lives of people, how will Christians sustain their faith and ensure that they have both the willingness and the power to carry the good news into the midst of a secular world as more than generalized doers of good deeds? Here, we detect an echo of some memorable words from Gene Heckathorn's journal nearly 50 years ago: "I think I can do more for people than all the 'do-gooders' I know."

Vesper Society entered the 21st century with a vision of a "compassionate world which protects human dignity and enhances human potential." Many humanitarian and philanthropic organizations across the globe share this aspiration, but is there more to be said by groups that understand and intentionally heed their callings as Christians in the world?

The current president of Vesper Society, Mary Olson Baich, stressed the importance of particularity in a 2005 pre-Kirchentag speech before the Global Economic Network, which met at the Evangelical Academy at Loccum, Germany. She noted the danger that a concern for universalism, for cooperation, might lead to a dehumanizing uniformity, a sinking to the lowest common denominator. That is doubtless part of the reason for the decline of the traditional church structures today – a concern to avoid a potentially offensive particularity.

To make Christianity into a simple do-goodism is a real danger, given the kind of radical life that Christ calls us to as Christians. "Taking up one's cross" and "turning the other cheek" are not part of the usual rubric of living ethically; normally, such behaviors would be viewed as rather strange. Gibbs himself, back in 1964, described in the last chapter of *God's Frozen People* the difficult life of the Christian layperson:

> To be a real layman ... is to undertake a hard and often uncertain pilgrimage. It is to struggle with a fog of ethical uncertainties, it is to face the misunderstanding of both friend and critic, it is to face accusations of being "disloyal," and "worldly," on the one hand – and yet on the other to be thought oddly scrupulous, something of a "sucker," someone to be exploited. And this is our true vocation.

The decline of the organized church in today's world is a crisis because it presents a real long-term danger for the Christian; it leaves us potentially adrift without moorings. It weakens the traditional structures by which for centuries the story has been told, the gospel proclaimed. It may lead us to be willing participants in a climate of generalized civic virtue rather than following The Way. It may lead us to separate Monday from Sunday, encouraging us to rely on culturally defined ethics instead of the grace of God in Christ. But this decline also presents us with a real opportunity.

Writing nearly 50 years ago in *God's Frozen People*, Gibbs recognized that "the present life of the church is not a full life," that "the life of the church is not adult, for what is excluded are the concerns of adult life." The weakening of traditional church structures is an opportunity to leave behind a Sunday school faith and truly become what Gibbs called "God's essential agents." We can leave behind our complaining about the church's lack of attention to the lives of most of the people of God in the real world and assume the responsibility ourselves to help each other be light and salt as Christians in daily life. The fact that the church may be invisible does not mean that the church is non-existent; it may just be embodied in the people of God everywhere in the world, as it was at the beginning, rather than being confined to a building at the corner. But if the church is to be sustained, if the people are to remain "of God" in the world, they must be nurtured in the faith. Gibbs counted himself among "those who are convinced that the Gospel is relevant to tomorrow, but in new ways." So how might the people of God be sustained in the faith in new ways?

The Daylesford participants recognized that the full expression of the ministry of the laity was yet to be realized. Their declaration acknowledged "more must be done to help Christians to discern and claim their ministries and to be affirmed, equipped, supported and empowered in them." Simultaneously, the declaration recognized that continued reliance on denominational structures to do this work was not enough, especially if those structures are becoming more peripheral to more people's lives. The Daylesford declaration committed participants to "work with each other, whenever practical, in developing and providing resources, offering events, doing research, sharing programs and learnings, and maintaining a network which will translate the rhetoric of Ministry in Daily Life into reality in the lives of our brothers and sisters in the faith."

The declaration echoed Gibbs' call to move "beyond chapter one." As he wrote in a 1984 essay,

> There are some disappointing signs that some denominations and laity centres are, as it were, stuck in 'Chapter One,' and not finding ways to explore the deep riches of Christian discipleship today. There is a certain tendency to respect rather glibly what are now, thank God, rather familiar phrases about 'Monday morning ministries' and 'enabling the laity' and 'faith in the workplace.' How can we achieve some real quality in our understanding of these great Christian truths?

In this stress on "quality," Gibbs recognized that doing more to support Christians in their ministries in daily life is not simply a quantitative matter of undertaking more programs or sponsoring more events. A different approach may be warranted, one that begins in reflection and conversation about the role of Christians in the intersection of faith and the world. And one largely carried out in and by groups not part of the organized church but very much part of the people of God.

Gibbs and Vesper Society rightly rejected the sentimental view that their vocation was limited to "the personal, loving, affectionate responsibilities to family, friends and neighbors." They wanted to exercise their power in the world, putting faith into action competently and effectively, for the common good. The American Lutheran theologian Joseph

Sittler expressed in *Gravity and Grace* a similar caution: "We are tempt-
ed to regard God primarily as a God for solitude and privacy and only
secondarily as a God for society. We have a God for my personal ache
and hurt, but no God for the problems of human life in the great
world." But neither Sittler nor Gibbs nor the founders of Vesper
Society wished to replace the God of personal devotion and worship
with a God interested in effective social structures but not in persons.
Their God was and is both personal and corporate, making persons as
well as social structures new. Their God redeems individuals as well as
the creation. Neither civil society nor ethics can redeem, and that may
well be forgotten in a world in which the organized church is relatively unimportant, unless individuals and other groups assume the
responsibility to say so and act out that faith in the world.

Certainly the claim of Norman Lear in 1987, quoted earlier, that
the role of the church as the focal point for personal values and public
mores has been assumed by the modern corporation, hardly seems sus-
tainable in light of recent corporate history. So if traditional church
structures are increasingly unable to be that focal point, while corporations cannot replace them for that purpose, what shall substitute? If
traditional church structures are either not willing or no longer strong
enough to call, nurture, and equip laypeople to be faithful Christians in
the world, what then? There will always be laypeople who hear the call
do God's work in the world, even when the church has walked away.
Daylesford apparently felt that Christians themselves, and organizations such as Vesper Society that are committed to ministry in daily life,
had to step up and fill the void.

In 2007 Oxford University Press published *God at Work: The History
and Promise of the Faith at Work Movement* by David W. Miller, who
directs the Princeton University Faith & Work Initiative. The book
includes a rather remarkable paragraph, referring to Mark Gibbs and
Vesper Society:

> As a result of the response to [Gibbs'] books, writings, and talks, he founded and led the Audenshaw Foundation, based in England, which was affiliated with the Vesper Society of San Leandro, California. Audenshaw gave Gibbs an institutional platform from which to carry out his lay ministry of faith and work. … Ironically, perhaps, what made Gibbs successful in his work – his engaging personality, abundant energy, networking, and single-minded focus on lay ministry – was what hurt the movement through its absence after he died. The Audenshaw Foundation and the Vesper Society soon lost energy and vision and closed down.

Despite the fact that Vesper Society certainly has not "closed down," it is the case that something changed at the Society and in the ministry in daily life movement generally and that Daylesford symbolizes some of that change. In the Daylesford declaration is the initial whisper of a call to the people of God to take the responsibility to *be* the people of God in the world rather than relying on the historic organized church structures. Perhaps to turn that whisper into a shout, what is required is that Vesper Society and like-minded organizations listen to and then act on these words of Gibbs, once again from *God's Frozen People*: "A truly corporate life means that responsible, adult people do things together from the necessity of their faith and because they are bound to one another in faith and love."

A particular, Christian focus requires, first of all, serious reflection, prayer, and conversation about the "more" the Daylesford declaration urges. Once again, it is helpful to listen carefully to Gibbs, who described the church as "essentially people living a life together: the people of God living the life of Christ." To this sentence from *God's Frozen People*, we might append the words – "and that life is lived *in the world*." What would it look like for individuals and groups to take up with renewed vigor the call to be the "people of God living the life of

Christ in the world"?

Gibbs offered some possibilities:

- *Education*: Gibbs believed in lifelong learning. He started his career as an educator and continued in that role until his death, teaching by writing, giving workshops and seminars, engaging people in deep conversations about important issues of faith and the world. For Christians, education has a particular end: to follow Christ, to "grow a deeper quality of Christian compassion, not withdrawn from but living in the midst of the pressures and ambiguities of our time," Gibbs said in his 1981 Vesper/Audenshaw lecture.

- *Mentoring*: Closely related to education, the main responsibility of senior lay leaders, Gibbs said, is to teach younger lay leaders how to navigate the world as people of faith. The "first duty" of veteran laypeople, Gibbs wrote in *God's Frozen People*, is "not to prop up the local institutional church, but to pass on their scarce skill, their all too rare professional knowledge – how to be a Christian [layperson] in their particular occupation."

- *Experimentation*: Gibbs said the task of the church ("the people of God living the life of Christ") is to engage in experiments that offer a way of life that is more satisfying because it is more demanding. Gibbs had in mind new patterns of church life and new modes of doing education, whether in the home, workplace or community.

We titled this book *Faith in the World*. That phrase never meant, for Gibbs or the founders of Vesper Society, faith in the world in lieu of God, or faith in a world without God, or faith in a world that thinks it has no need of God. It did and does mean living a life of faith in the world that is, after all, God's world. And it means living a life of faith in today's world, not in yesterday's. It means moving beyond complaining that the church doesn't "get it" to stepping up and assuming our responsibilities ourselves. How can we do that?

We suggest that readers reflect upon the following questions for their faith communities and organizations:

- What is the larger calling of this organization and of the individuals within the organization?

- How is that calling derived from and resonant with our faith – rooted in the Gospel, drawing strength from Word and Sacraments – and how does our work remain so without being dependent upon the institutional church or, conversely, captive to culture?

- In seeking a fuller realization of the ministry of the laity, how could we leverage current interest in "spirituality," "servant-leadership" and "civil society" to lead others into serious reflection on their vocation in the world as people of a particular faith?

- How could our group provide deeper educational opportunities to help laypeople discern and claim their ministries in the world, as the Lutheran Church in America program "Word and Witness" did in the 1970s (though it emphasized personal relationships rather than societal structures)?

- How do we encourage mentoring to ensure that active faith in the world persists from generation to generation?

- What experiments could we undertake to emphasize the connection between faith practices and desirable social ends, as in the Vesper Society-sponsored

Masangane Treatment Program or Dialogue for Peaceful Change, for example?

• What can our organization do to collaborate with other similarly motivated groups to support, deepen, and broaden the efforts of all?

While Daylesford led to the conviction that the ministry in daily life movement could chart its own course, what will ensure that that course is grounded and anchored in the Christian faith rather than in a generalized impulse to work for the common good? The long-term challenge for Christians is how to remain rooted in the Gospel if the church is no longer central. Doing that will require a new intentionality in the work of such organizations as Vesper Society – not to take the place of the congregation but to recognize that the church has always been the people of God, not an entity with a corporate headquarters. Figuring out how to develop such a new intentionality in a way that proclaims the good news and enables Christians to carry that good news into the world without passing judgment or being narrowly exclusionary will not be easy. But our reflections and conversations during the writing of this book have led us to conclude that this is the inevitable and essential task of the people of God.

At about the same time that Vesper Society was founded and Gibbs' *God's Frozen People* was published, the theologian Joseph Sittler was writing about the danger of separating the first and second articles of the Creed – of separating Creation from Redemption, of disconnecting the created world from God's act of salvation in Christ. In words that resonate with Gibbs and the intention of Vesper Society, Sittler wrote in the 1966 book *The Anguish of Preaching* that this

almost complete severance of the realm of redemption from the realm of creation ... moralized Christian thought and seals within private piety and an individualistic understanding of obedience the world-restoring

intention of the gospel of God. It encourages an understanding of church as a gathered coterie of the
redeemed who now celebrate the benefits of their
redemption, and it detaches the acknowledging company from positive stance and action within the world ...

Mark Gibbs and the founders of Vesper Society would surely have said
to Sittler's words, "Amen!"

This theological understanding of the essential nature of the work
of the people of God in the world that keeps God's activity in creation
united with God's activity in redemption is powerfully supportive of all
that the convergence of Gibbs and Vesper Society was about and why
continuing their work is so important. We hope our words convey
enough of the power of that historic convergence to serve as catalyst for
further reflection on the meaning of faith in the world. We hope that
even tomorrow, the people of God may live the life of Christ in the
world, sustained by grace and empowered by each other as the church
– the successors of Mark Gibbs and the founders of Vesper Society.

❖ Appendix ❖

The following essay appeared in Vesper Exchange, *first quarter, 1979. Gibbs' analysis of power — a theme he explored in greater depth in his final book,* Christians With Secular Power *(Philadelphia: Fortress Press, 1981) — is just as relevant today. So too is his call for "competent citizens."*

"That the Good May Be Clever"
By Mark Gibbs

This is a most uncomfortable year. The shifts of power in the Far East and in Africa, the dangerous uncertainties in Iran and in Saudi Arabia: these demand that we shall lift our sights from personal and family preoccupations and face again some very unpleasant realities in world politics.

Citizens of Britain or of the Netherlands, of Israel or of Poland, those who live in most of the smaller countries of the world can but watch and hope that apocalyptic wars may be averted, that gasoline may be available, that the leaders of the great powers will neither by criminal intention nor by negligence and sloppiness blunder into major war. Citizens of the American Republic have a deeper responsibility. Their country is one of the major world powers — surely, even now, the most powerful of all. Their elected President and Congress must carry the burden of the world's peace and stability upon their shoulders.

World Power Politics

To understand the dangerous world we now live in, we have to learn or relearn the basic facts of power politics. (To learn such facts is not, of course, necessarily to approve of them.) There are four major kinds of power: military, economic, political and religious or ideological. We may very much dislike even thinking about the use and misuse of some of these kinds of power; but to pretend that they do not exist is prissy and foolhardy. We need again to listen to and argue with such twentieth century prophets as Bertrand Russell, Reinhold Niebuhr and Henry Kissinger.

In particular, good, decent, moderate citizens – faithful writers and readers of *Vesper Exchange* – we have, I suspect, to rethink our understanding of the power of belief in the modern world. Some kinds of religious or ideological fanaticism are still very strong indeed; and they are mostly doing great harm rather than great good. The resurgence of some kinds of Islamic beliefs in Iran or Pakistan, the intolerant Christianities in South Africa or Northern Ireland, the extremist Judaisms in Israel, the fundamentalist Marxist faiths in Africa or Cambodia – these can be damnably powerful and cruel beliefs. We may claim, no doubt, that purer versions of such faiths ought to generate a true love for humanity and for our immediate neighbors; but the hard fact is that in the twentieth as in the seventeenth century these corrupted beliefs persecute, tyrannize, and poison both national and international communities.

Military power seems easier to understand; though we are inclined to be too squeamish to reflect about the dreadful potential and also the limited utility of nuclear arms. World atomic war must be so appalling that its possibility will always pose a ghastly dilemma to politicians. How much of a defeat ought we to accept before we use the bombs?

Economic power is sometimes more difficult to assess. Anybody can see the unpleasant fact that the Western nations – especially of course the United States – now enjoy an economic system which depends on high oil usage, which in turn depends on oil imports from the Middle East. What is more difficult to analyze is the extent to which much of the world (including those same Middle East oil nations) are themselves now dependant on a style of economic and technological development which ties them to the West – or to the Soviet Union bloc, the only other source as yet of major industrial know-how. Political power – the democratic or authoritarian organization of peoples and of their military and economic strength – has unfortunately once more been downgraded in the eyes of many voters. To be a politician is a dangerous, ambiguous but (as Robert Kennedy was fond of saying) "an honorable profession"; and though many may question the stances and policies of a man like President Carter, none can deny that to be a "born again" president is as fine an ambition as to be a dedicated preacher.

Must the Saints Be Outwitted?

Indeed, questions of vocation, of honor, of decency, of morality are by no means at all to be excluded from a grimly realistic analysis of power in the world of 1979. The point is that intelligence and virtue and hard thinking have to go together: "if only the good were clever" is a heartfelt cry from the past centuries where the ordinary people have had to suffer simple saints and very skillful sinners. Here the thousands of churches and synagogues in the United States are particularly important. It is unfortunately true that many members of American religious bodies – including some of their most popular leaders and pastors – are still inclined to avert their eyes from disturbing world news bulletins, and to concentrate on "manageable" questions of personal and family morality. Such a purely private faith is as dangerous as a fanatically political one. This is exactly the time when we must be encouraged to face the unpleasant facts of world affairs, when we must learn not only to be well-meaning, but also competent citizens.

Mark Gibbs delivered the following keynote address to the Lutheran Church in America's LAOS Theologians' Colloquium in New York City May 23, 1982.

"No More Spiritual Babies: The Development of a Strong Laity" By Mark Gibbs

It is a pleasure and an honour to be here. Both my colleagues in the Audenshaw Foundation and I myself have greatly appreciated the chance to learn from the Lutheran Church in America and its seminaries during my visits over the past few years. It is however with some trepidation that I face the serried ranks of Lutheran scholars here assembled, especially in view of the two special tasks which Nelvin Vos has laid before me.

It is of enormous importance that your church – that every church – develop a strong theology of the *laos*, of the whole People of God (of whom of course 1 percent are clergy and 99 percent laity). It will be a very great prize if we can understand and put into practice the calling and the potential of this 99 percent laity. Indeed this is, I claim, the key to the effective service and witness and mission of the Church of Jesus Christ for the 21st century. No buildings, no structures, no mergers of churches, no "new church" will be effective without it.

There Has Been Progress

Yes, there has been great progress in recent years. Nelvin Vos requested firstly that I should try to add an *ecumenical dimension* to this colloquium, and I am very happy to respond. I am myself an Anglican, but I am always thankful that I learned to think ecumenically from a very early age. I could never quite accept that God ever reserved all his truth for the inspiration of white male Anglican clergy from Oxford or Canterbury! And we must remember too that Lutherans have not always thought ecumenically in the past. The wonderful fact about the

development of the laity in the last thirty years is that it has happened
all over the Church of Jesus Christ, and all over the world. From
Quakers and Baptists to Roman Catholics. From Boise, Idaho, to
Blantyre, Malawi. And this has included both "formal" (church member) Christians and "informal" (less affiliated) Christians. We have all
begun to recover the New Testament doctrine of the common calling of
all the People of God, to a royal priesthood (1 Peter 2:9), to an adult
Christian maturity (Ephesians 4).

- Consider the intense development of a social dimension to the faith of the laity which is represented by
  the *Sojourners* movement, or by the Reformed traditions of, say, Calvin College.

- The Roman Catholic bishops' statement about the
  laity, *Called and Gifted*. Edwina Gateley wrote an
  article for *Laity Exchange* entitled "The Laity Have
  Been in Exile." Yes, and they are now claiming their
  rightful place in the Catholic Church.

- The Baptist World Alliance (which includes the
  Southern Baptists) has recently established a world
  committee on the laity, and George Peck from the
  Andover-Newton Theological School has reported
  some extraordinary common thinking at their first
  meeting in Puerto Rico.

You will know that Audenshaw and Vesper Society are establishing
the first Laity Research Center in North America, at the Lutheran
School of Theology in Chicago. As we begin to assemble the first materials for this center, from the documents and reports of the last
half-century, I am more than ever impressed by the progress made since
the Second World War.

Half-Believers in the Laity?

But Nelvin Vos' second instruction to me was that I must be *intellectually fair and honest* in speaking to you tonight. And so I must put it to you that despite these changes and advances, a great many of our church leaders and thinkers, in North America as elsewhere, only half-believe in the vocation of the laity. There is still a great deal of tokenism about this. And such half-believing, such half-hearted assent, is dangerous spiritually, theologically, and intellectually. This colloquium is of course an intellectual event (though I hope this does not mean it will be a dull one!) And I think we must recall tonight that Christian intellectuals must be servant intellectuals, and we must put strenuous efforts into helping our fellow church members and our church institutions to understand the enormous importance and the considerable complexity of a theology of the *laos* and of the laity. I have recently written a short paper, "The Marks of a Seminary That Takes the Laity Seriously," and you will have copies, so that I do not need to go over all the conclusions I came to after visiting some of your seminaries. But let me give you some examples of the thorough and indeed ruthless rethinking which I am convinced we must come to.

(1) All are called?

Do we really believe this, and do our curricula and discussions reflect this belief? The laity, just as much as the ordained? Blue-collar laity, women, young, elderly, illiterate? All gifted? All potential ministers? All to be legitimated and affirmed and supported in their ministries? (And do our liturgies strongly say these things?)

(2) All called for all of our days and years?

We understand – you in the United Sates particularly understand – the importance of the *Sunday* ministries of the laity; and indeed many parishes and congregations could not survive without them. (But how far are Sunday worship services really a true partnership between the ordained and unordained ministers?) The LAOS movement, especially influenced by the fine work of Bill Diehl, has done much to emphasize the importance of *Monday's* ministries – not only personal integrity at work but also the ministries in the powerful and sometimes corrupt structures of daily life. By no means do all seminary curricula reflect these concerns. And I suspect we are still further behind in understanding and theologizing about what I have called "*Saturday's Ministries*" – the involvement of Christians in the structures of leisure – vacations, tourism, entertainments, sports, television.

(3) Both laity and clergy called?

Yes, we agree in principle. But it still seems very difficult to foster true and fruitful partnerships between ordained and unordained ministers. Certainly this is often the fault of uncommitted and/or docile laity; but I do not think we have sufficiently examined the psychology of clergy/laity relationships. It is impossible to have a true partnership if one partner (the pastor) always expects to be the senior partner! And if he/she takes an attitude that the laity are normally weak and in need of spiritual strength which he/she must give. Pat Drake of the Alban Institute has written a perceptive article in which she insists "I am not sick!"; and Renae Hyer, the first woman vice-president of the Bank of America and a very faithful Lutheran, wrote a piece for *Laity Exchange* in which she pointed out that her pastor was admirable in helping her when she was down, and needed counseling, but was uneasy with her when she felt "strong" and was enjoying her secular responsibilities. John Bluck, of the World Council of Churches, has pointed out that we have at least some "theologically equipped laypeople who won't accept pastoral paternalism and intellectual mollycoddling."

How can clergy leaders – from the Pope down – learn to *listen* to laity, and how can clergy accept and encourage the ministries of the laity outside church and parish structures?

(4) A serious investment in the development of the laity?

To some extent the question as to whether we shall have a strong, theologically literate laity in the future is now a dollars and cents question. We have had so much talking about the laity. If we are to move beyond amiable rhetoric, we need more of our church budgets allocated for laity development. We need more scholarships for young laity and grants for their self-education (just as we have for clergy). (The United Church of Canada has some excellent schemes here which are worth investigating.) And we need – like our Evangelical friends – to encourage the laity to invest in their own Christian future. Samuel Lipman wrote in a recent issue of *Commentary* about the development of music in the Bay Area: They had the good fortune to find in San Francisco an aristocracy of German Jews, for whom the support of culture was the road to Heaven. If only the Christian laity had such devoted patrons!

The Time Is Critical

I make no apology for cultivating a certain holy impatience about these matters, for in the American churches – and particularly among you Lutherans who are now establishing a New Church – we have opportunities for laity development which may not easily recur again in the next half-century. The days of a mass of sheepish, ethnically motivated laity are fast disappearing. If we do not offer the laity chances for developing a mature faith, and a critical loyalty to their churches, then in the United States as in Canada and Europe they will quietly "vote with their feet," and in Hans Küng's words "… the silent mass withdrawal from the Church will continue." Yet I am sure that Lutherans, especially, still have a fine chance to lead in the American scene, if only you can work on the right priorities in developing our common vocation – clergy and laity together. I think especially of a proper Christian toughness, and of an understanding of the costs of discipleship in modern America. Our vocation is bound to be – at the least – an uncomfortable one: it has to speak of the Gospel. But we still have a chance to develop an adult, mature, strong, dogged, determined, able laity which "having done all may still stand." No more sheep, no more spiritual babies, but strong disciples.

❀ Selected Bibliography ❀

Books by Mark Gibbs:

A Man to Be Reckoned With: The Story of Reinold von Thadden-Trieglaff. By Werner Huhne. Edited and translated by Mark Gibbs. London: SCM Press, 1962.

God's Frozen People. With T. Ralph Morton. Philadelphia: Westminster Press, 1964.

God's Lively People. With T. Ralph Morton. Philadelphia: Westminster Press, 1971.

Christians With Secular Power. A Laity Exchange Book. Philadelphia: Fortress Press, 1981.

All Are Called: Towards a Theology of the Laity. London: Church House Publishing, 1985. Two essays: "Ministries Outside the Parish" and "The Spiritual Growth of the Laity."

Laity Exchange Books edited by Mark Gibbs and published by Fortress Press:

Mouw, Richard J. *Called to Holy Worldliness,* 1980.

Diehl, William E. *Thank God, It's Monday!* 1982.

Jenkins, Daniel. *Christian Maturity and Christian Success,* 1982.

Vos, Nelvin. *Seven Days A Week: Faith in Action,* 1985.

❧ About the Authors ❧

NELVIN VOS is Emeritus Professor of English at Muhlenberg College. He served on the Board of Directors of Vesper Society from 1999-2004, the latter two years as chair. The author of *Monday's Ministries: The Ministry of the Laity*, Vos has been active in the laity movement since the 1970s as a writer and retreat leader. After Mark Gibbs' death, Vos served several years as editor of Fortress Press' Laity Exchange book series and editor of *Laity Exchange*, a Vesper Society publication.

DANIEL PRYFOGLE is a journalist, teacher, and consultant. He is principal of The Signal Hill Company, a leadership and communications consultancy that serves churches and nonprofit organizations. From 2004-2008, he was an instructor in the Faith-Based Leadership Institute, an ecumenical leadership development program founded by Vesper Society for health and human service leaders. He has consulted with the Society since 2004.

MELVIN GEORGE is a retired professor of mathematics and administrator in several higher education institutions. During 1985-1994, he was president of St. Olaf College, a Lutheran (ELCA) institution in Northfield, Minn. He has twice been interim president of the University of Missouri System and has been an active member of the Board of Directors of Vesper Society since 1998, serving as chair for two years.

Made in the USA
Charleston, SC
26 September 2011